Theos Friends' Programme

Theos is a religion and society think tank which seeks to inform and influence public opinion about the role of faith and belief in society.

We were launched in November 2006 with the support of the Archbishop of Canterbury, Dr Rowan Williams and the Cardinal Archbishop of Westminster, Cardinal Cormac Murphy-O'Connor.

We provide

- high-quality research, reports and publications;
- an events programme;
- news, information and analysis to media companies, parliamentarians and other opinion formers.

We can only do this with your help!

Theos Friends receive complimentary copies of all Theos publications, invitations to selected events and monthly email bulletins.

Theos Associates receive all the benefits of Friends and in addition are invited to attend an exclusive annual dinner with the Theos Director and team.

If you would like to become a Friend or an Associate, detach or photocopy the form below, and send it with a cheque to Theos for the relevant amount. Thank you.

Alternatively, it's very simply to become a friend or Associate via our website www.theosthinktank.co.uk/support

Yes, I would like to help change public opinion!
I enclose a cheque payable to Theos for: ☐ **£60** (Friend) ☐ **£300** (Associate)

☐ Please send me information on how to give by standing order/direct debit

Name _____

Address _____

_____ Postcode _____

Email _____

Tel _____

Data Protection Theos will use your personal data to
If you prefer not to receive this information please tic

By completing you are consenting to receiving commu
Theos will not pass on your details to any third party.

Please return this form to:
Theos | 77 Great Peter Street | London | SW1P
S: 97711 D: 36701

Theos

Theos – clear thinking on religion and society

Theos is a Christian think tank working in the area of religion, politics and society. We aim to inform debate around questions of faith and secularism and the related subjects of values and identity. We were launched in November 2006, and our first report *'Doing God'; a Future for Faith in the Public Square,* written by Nick Spencer, examined the reasons why faith will play an increasingly significant role in public life.

what Theos stands for

In our post-secular age, interest in spirituality is increasing across Western culture. We believe that it is impossible to understand the modern world without an understanding of religion. We also believe that much of the debate about the role and place of religion has been unnecessarily emotive and ill-informed. We reject the notion of any possible 'neutral' perspective on these issues.

what Theos works on

Theos conducts research, publishes reports, and runs debates, seminars and lectures on the intersection of religion, politics and society in the contemporary world. We also provide regular comment for print and broadcast media. Recent areas of analysis include multiculturalism, Christian education, religious liberty and the future of religious representation in the House of Lords. Future areas of focus will include questions of values in economic policy and practice and the role of religion in international affairs.

what Theos provides

In addition to our independently driven work, Theos provides research, analysis and advice to individuals and organisations across the private, public and not-for-profit sectors. Our unique position within the think tank sector means that we have the capacity to develop proposals that carry values – with an eye to demonstrating what really works.

what Theos believes

Theos was launched with the support of the Archbishop of Canterbury and the Cardinal Archbishop of Westminster, but it is independent of any particular denomination. We are an ecumenical Christian organisation, committed to the belief that religion in general and Christianity in particular has much to offer for the common good of society as a whole. We are committed to the traditional creeds of the Christian faith and draw on social and political thought from a wide range of theological traditions. We also work with many non-Christian and non-religious individuals and organisations.

How to think about religious freedom

Nick Spencer

Published by Theos in 2014
© Theos

ISBN 978-0-9574743-4-5̶ 2

Some rights reserved – see copyright licence for details
For further information and subscription details please contact:

Theos
Licence Department
77 Great Peter Street
London
SW1P 2EZ

T 020 7828 7777
E hello@theosthinktank.co.uk
www.theosthinktank.co.uk

contents

foreword

Theos is concerned with religion in public life: how it is perceived, how we talk about it and ultimately how we live together well, despite our differences. Over the last few years a strong narrative has been developing that 'religious rights' can't help but come to blows with 'human rights', and that the only way to deal with this is in the courts. A series of high-profile cases, various campaigns by secularist groups and an increasing sense of nervousness among many in the workplace have made this narrative ever more available that if narrative were true, our hopes of living together well would be definitely under threat.

We don't believe it is. Therefore, in late 2012, Theos published a volume of essays entitled Religion and Law. It offered insights from 16 leading legal experts on a variety of knotty subjects around the topic: religious symbols, minority religious orders, religious discrimination, religious freedom, the relationship between religion and human rights, and similar issues. Intended to shed light in an arena usually marked by heat, the volume formed part one of a larger Theos project on religion and law. Nick Spencer, the volume's editor, noted in its introduction that some readers might be frustrated at its lack of directionality, intended, as it was, to clarify rather than to solve. He promised in this introduction what he has now delivered, part two of the project, a "guidebook" for how we might navigate the increasingly confused and confusing landscape of religion and law in the UK today.

This guidebook is unapologetically Christian, meaning its foundation and internal logic rest on a commitment to Christian scripture and theological reflection. That may alienate those who do not share those commitments and presuppositions but, as Theos frequently notes, everyone engages with these vexed ethical, social and legal issues with their own commitments and presuppositions – there is no view from nowhere – and it is better, therefore, that when people do engage with these issues they do so authentically (drawing on their own commitments rather than on other people's) and openly (showing their workings, the ideological wiring under the bonnet so to speak). This is what this essay does.

Beginning with seven core principles, the essay then applies these to some of the most interesting and practical legal/religious questions we face. In doing this, Nick offers a way to think about religious freedom that is authentically and explicitly Christian but not, it is hoped, so confessional as to make it irrelevant to those who are not Christian. As he observes early on, very often Christian and non-Christian, indeed non-religious, people will come to similar conclusions about the question of religious freedom, just travelling via different intellectual paths to get there.

The questions surrounding religious freedom, like the wider set of questions around political freedom – indeed like any important question concerning how we live together – will always be susceptible to disagreement, based on the different concepts of the good that rub shoulders in any plural society. We should not be disappointed with this or even surprised. The task is to work through and accommodate those differences authentically, openly and fairly and I believe this report will contribute to that task.

Elizabeth Oldfield
Director, Theos

introduction

The Shouwang – or "Watchtower" – Church is one of China's many independent house churches. Not a member of the officially sanctioned Three-Self Patriotic Movement, the Church has been ejected from rented venues (on account of government pressure on landlords) and has also been prevented from gaining access to a building it purchased. Forced to meet outside, members have been detained and questioned by police, a number being forced to sign a declaration saying they would not attend the church again. Some of their church's leaders have been put under house arrest. When the New Tree Church, another Beijing house church, sent some of its members to stand in solidarity with Shouwang Church, their pastor was detained for 48 hours on "suspicion of disrupting the public order".

China is a one-party atheist state. Although the constitution theoretically protects religious freedom – Article 36 states that "no state organ, public organization or individual may compel citizens to believe in, or not to believe in, any religion; nor may they discriminate against citizens who believe in, or do not believe in, any religion" – it also says that "no one may make use of religion to engage in activities that disrupt public order, impair the health of citizens or interfere with the educational system of the state." Members of the ruling Communist Party must be atheist. All places of worship are under the administrative control of the Bureau of Religious Affairs. Religious bodies and religious affairs may not recognise any foreign authority, including the Papacy.

The position of Christians in China today is better than it has been for much of the twentieth century.[1] It is also rather better than the conditions of Christians in neighbouring North Korea, where despite Constitutional Articles to the contrary,[2] churches are closed, Bibles banned, believers imprisoned, and pastors killed.[3] Yet the Chinese example serves to remind us that religious freedom within atheist states, even those as rapidly modernising as China, is a live issue.

The Chinese example is useful in other ways, too. In the same way as it invites atheists who talk about bishops in the House of Lords as if it were some horrendous scar on the face of liberty and justice ("Only Britain and Iran…") to get a little perspective, it invites those Christians who talk about persecution at home to do the same. When Christians are banned from meeting or live in fear of attack, or are barred from public office, or don't have access to the Bible, or risk imprisonment or torture, then it is the right time to talk about persecution. Christians in Britain have not experienced these things. They are not persecuted.

There is another, perhaps less obvious perspective that the Chinese example offers for an analysis of religious freedom in Britain. The conditions faced by Christians in China (or North Korea) allow us to ask a provocative question that might help clarify our thinking: why are the things outlined above wrong?

At first blush, this is just self-evident. It is *obvious* that depriving someone of their ability to read the Bible, to pray, to assemble, to worship, or to hold political office is wrong. It is even more obvious that mentally or physically punishing them for attempting to do any of these things is even more reprehensible.

However, too often we simply assume such behaviour is wrong without thinking about why. We reach for an easy phrase from the shelf – usually 'violation of their human rights' – and imagine that is somehow adequate to the task of thinking about religious freedom.

Taking the time to answer this 'why' question from the bottom up may help us generate a commitment to religious freedom that is true to Christian thought and commitments, rather than one that simply apes whatever secular reasoning happens to be popular at the moment.[4]

Moreover, going through this exercise may help us answer further, more contentious questions. Knowing *why* we value religious freedom should give us some guidance as to *what* precisely we should value and *how* we should value it, even if it will not decide such questions for us. In the words of the legal scholar, Jeremy Waldron:

> the study of concepts like *law*, and *freedom*, and *power*, and *democracy* cannot be undertaken in a normative vacuum. Unless, for example, we have some idea of why it might *matter*, why it might be thought a matter of *concern* whether something is a law or not, we cannot sensibly choose among rival conceptions of this concept.[5]

This is a particularly important task right now. The religion and law landscape in Britain has changed considerably and very rapidly over the last generation. This is partly because the religious landscape is more varied and complex than it was 30 years ago, but mainly because the legislative landscape is very different, much more crowded and now dominated by two huge features – the Human Rights Act 1998 (particularly Article 9 providing for freedom of thought, religion and conscience[6]) and the Equality Act 2010 (which protects from discrimination 'religion or belief' alongside seven other 'protected characteristics'[7] – that were largely absent 20 years ago. According to legal scholar Russell Sandberg, what was once the default position of a "passive tolerance of religious difference" has been superseded "by the prescriptive regulation of religion and the active promotion of religious liberty as a right."[8]

The result has been an unprecedented juridification of religion (indeed, arguably an unprecedented juridification of life) over the last fifteen years, a so-called 'legal explosion'. The law has come to regulate an ever-growing number and range of activities; conflicts are more likely to be solved by or with reference to law, and "people increasingly tend to think of themselves and others as legal subjects".[9] Whether or not this is a good thing (though it is hard to find people who think it is good as opposed to, say, a necessity), it constitutes a real and significant change in the world of religion and law, one that requires careful and sustained analysis.

As if this were not complex enough, that juridification has taken on a newly international flavour, as the European Court of Human Rights has become the court of last appeal for many cases. "English religion law is now shaped more by international norms than it has been at any time since the medieval period."[10] This is not a problem in itself, although the British public's deep antipathy to many things European certainly adds some colour and noise to the discussion. However, as Lord Sumption (among others) has pointed out, the European Convention for the Protection of Human Rights and Fundamental Freedoms, because it is a so-called 'living instrument', has had a pronounced tendency towards converting political questions into legal ones.[11]

> The effect of this kind of judicial lawmaking...is to take many contentious issues which would previously have been regarded as questions for political debate, administrative discretion or social convention and transform them into questions of law to be resolved by an international judicial tribunal... In reality...the Human Rights Act involves the transfer of part of an essentially legislative power to another body.[12]

This is certainly not a problem limited to issues of religious freedom (witness the on-going and bad-tempered debate about prisoner voting rights) but it does add a further complexity – and passion – to the already vexed – and passionate – debates over religious freedom.

The result of all this, therefore, is that the need to think carefully about freedom in general, and religious freedom in particular, while never absent in any generation, is particularly acute today.

This essay explores the why, what and how of religious freedom. It is divided into two parts. The first outlines seven principles by means of which we can think about religious freedom. These are drawn from Christian scripture and theology and are intended to offer a – *not the* – set of guidelines by means of which readers might think more clearly about religious freedom.

It will be clear from this that the intended audience is primarily a Christian one, those who recognise the authority of scripture and the relevance of Christian traditions. If this seems needlessly restrictive, it is worth noting that everyone comes at the issue of freedom (and equality, and legality, and so forth) from some particular position.

Attempts to construct political, economic or legal systems that are independent of ethical frameworks and commitments, and the beliefs that underpin them, are doomed to failure. Indeed, more ominously, they are liable to smuggle in conceptions of the good like so much ideological contraband. Concepts such as 'choice', 'liberty', 'rationality', and 'autonomy', to take four of the most popular contemporary terms, may seem self-evident and universally-held, but are, in fact, neither, often grounded in a narrow, liberal, secular view of human beings and of human flourishing. There is no view from nowhere and pretending otherwise is at best lazy and at worst a covert power-grab for public authority without doing the hard work of public persuasion first.

It may be – indeed it is highly likely – that people of very different religious and moral presuppositions end up supporting similar legal positions and decisions. However, it is important that they do so in accordance with their own presuppositions, in other words with authenticity and integrity. For example, it is perfectly possible that Christian and secularist believers will agree that the state should not punish blasphemy, or that it should permit and fund church schools. But they are equally likely – *indeed they should* – do so for subtly different reasons, the conclusions arrived at from different starting points and via different routes.

This essay is an attempt to navigate the (mine)field of religious freedom in a way that is authentic to the Christian faith. That means that while there are unlikely to be very many secular fellow-travellers, there should be some secularists who are waiting for us at the conclusions we reach.

The principles in part one are necessarily brief. The essay is neither exhaustive nor academic but, rather, intended to be accessible, digestible and, above all, helpful. In the light of that objective, part two explores what these principles might entail, what they might look like, in the real world. By drawing on a number of legal cases – a limited number, as the field is vast and rapidly developing – it shows where an authentically Christian approach to religious freedom might take you.

A number of people have been instrumental in helping get this volume off the ground. In addition to my colleagues Elizabeth Oldfield, Paul Bickley, Alanna Harris and Ben Ryan,

David McIlroy, Julian Rivers and Jonathan Chaplin offered helpful comments on an earlier draft. The essay is the second part of a project funded by the Hinchley Charitable Trust and the Tufton Trust, the first part of which comprised sixteen essays by leading legal and philosophical thinkers in this area, exploring a range of different aspects of the religion and law debate. It, like this, is available from Theos (www.theosthinktank.co.uk) in the hope that intelligent and informed reflection will help us navigate a plain that seems daily to be swept with confused alarms of struggle and flight.

principles of religious freedom

1.1 'spirituality' is key to human identity, and requires recognition and respect

Human beings are made in the image of, and intended for relationship with, their creator. This is a fundamental conviction of all Christian denominations, and the keystone of Christian anthropology. In the opening words of the Catholic Catechism, "God…in a plan of sheer goodness freely created man [sic] to make him share in his own blessed life… He calls man to seek him, to know him, [and] to love him with all his strength."

The richness of this language is characteristic of Catholic thought but the belief is shared across denominations, albeit often expressed in more spare terms. Thus, the Westminster Shorter Catechism of 1640 opens with the following famous question and answer: "Q. What is the chief end of man? A. Man's chief end is to glorify God, and to enjoy him forever."

These doctrinal statements are deeply rooted within the Christian scriptures, from the early chapters of Genesis in which the human condition is marked by alienation and exile from God, through to the eschatological visions of both Old[13] and New[14] Testaments in which disparate peoples are gathered to God, who "will wipe away every tear from their eyes." This is not an eschatological vision in the sense that it is confined to the end of time, a state of affairs for which we can only wait passively. Christian thought, rather, speaks of 'realised eschatology', in which the promised ultimate state of affairs is present and can be cultivated and enjoyed here and now (thus, Jesus' prayer: "thy kingdom come/ on earth as in heaven").

Humans are famously made in *imago dei,* the image of God, a phrase that has been open to more (and more varied) interpretation than perhaps any other in Christian history. Among the more convincing of these interpretations is the idea that the God in whose image humans are made is irreducibly relational, a relationship into which humans are invited. In the words of Pope Benedict XVI's encyclical, *Caritas in Veritate,* "The Trinity is absolute unity insofar as the three divine Persons are pure relationality…God desires to incorporate us into this reality of communion as well: 'that they may be one even as we are one.'"[15] In the most profound way, to borrow the words of Orthodox theologian John Ziziolous, being is communion.[16]

This is central to the Christian understanding and defence of freedom. True freedom is predicated on recognising that humans live, as it were, in three dimensions, and that human nature only finds its fulfilment in communion with God. To prohibit this is effectively to circumscribe the human, to limit our horizons and force us to live in two dimensions, replacing our spiritual ends, our capacity to be "self-transcendent", with something that is exclusively material and finite.

> *True freedom is predicated on recognising that humans live in three dimensions and that human nature only finds its fulfilment in communion with God.*

It is also important in so far as beginning elsewhere for a defence and articulation of religious freedom is liable to flatten that freedom, to order it solely according to the criteria that are salient to and recognised by secular definitions of freedom. The *details* of religious freedom may not be qualitatively different from other freedoms, involving freedom of conscience, speech, association etc., but they are conceptually different, justified by different considerations, in particular a different understanding of what it means to be fully human.

1.2 religious belief cannot be neatly detached from religious practice

Historically in Britain, this central plank of religious freedom has been conceived in a somewhat restricted way, not so much for political as for theological reasons. The freedom "to seek [God], to know him, to love him with all his strength" has been understood as, and often limited to, freedom of conscience and freedom of worship; the freedom to choose between different (at first Protestant, then Christian, then religious, and finally any) creeds, and then to conduct religious services, or not, according to that choice.

There were (understandable) historical reasons for this conception, based, as it was, on a particular Protestant idea that Christianity (and by association religion) was primarily about believing the right thing and "worshipping" (narrowly conceived) in the right way.

This conception of what religion entails and demands is, however, all but unrecognisable in most other places and times on earth. Moreover, it is also firmly at odds with both the biblical and ecclesiological witness within Christian history. The worship of God in the Old Testament was a thoroughly public and thoroughly material activity, whose practices and demands were originally set out in law.

Because Jesus was relaxed about the precise demands of those traditions, and because St Paul placed a particular emphasis on salvation by faith, there have been streams within Christian thought that have sought to dematerialise religious commitment. Protestant reformers, reading into the rich material culture of late mediaeval Christianity the same criticism that St Paul was supposedly levelling at first-century Israel, bequeathed to English and Scottish Christianity a strong emphasis on inwardness as the sole legitimate mark of authenticity. Outward manifestations were, at best, incidental and, at worst, idolatrous.

However, this was never the sole strand with British Christianity, not simply because the Church of England integrated both Catholic and Reformed traditions, but because the doctrine of (the goodness of) creation is central to Christian thought, affirmed in the Old Testament and confirmed, by the resurrection, in the New.

> Whatever else the earliest church was, it was not a private society dedicated to right thinking.

Similarly, whatever else the earliest church was, it was not a private society dedicated to right thinking. The early chapters of Acts, which sketch out the life of the nascent church, see the first believers as engaging in acts of public proclamation, public assembly, public action, and, when pressed, public confrontation.[17] Being religious meant much more than believing religious things. It involved some serious, and costly, material commitments.

Recovering the irreducible materiality of spirituality is important, partly because it is true to the doctrine of creation and resurrection; partly because many of the legal issues in this area relate to 'manifestations' of belief; and partly because it provides a framework by means of which other non-Christian religions can be engaged on their own terms, rather than imposing a more narrowly Protestant conception of 'faith' on them.

1.3 religious freedom means freedom to adhere to, exercise and choose between all religions and none

These two principles – the need (1) to respect innate human spirituality and (2) to recognise that religious belief cannot be neatly detached from religious practice – are critical to the way we think about religious freedom.

Taken in isolation, however, they could be interpreted as a call for the state to secure *Christian* freedom (i.e. religious freedom for Christians alone) rather than (or even at the expense of) *religious* freedom (i.e. for other and non-religious believers). Do the Christian principles for religious freedom point only towards 'Christian freedom' narrowly understood?

The answer to this is an emphatic no. A balanced and authentic reading of Christian scripture and tradition shows that the Old Testament model, on which this limited understanding religious freedom was historically based, is, when read alone and out of context, inadequate. Quite apart from the fact the religious stipulations in the Old Testament law apply to Israel alone (the Israelites had no mandate to coerce the religious commitment of other nations), it is simply not possible to draw a direct line of between the religious laws of covenanted Israel and modern nation states (despite many such states wanting to claim Israel's mantle). The New Testament gets in the way.

This New Testament teaching on religious freedom is complex but, for our purposes, one key point demands emphasis. In the New Testament, the symbol of political authority is the sword.[18] This can be used justly, as St Paul envisages in his letter to the church in Rome, but it is, nonetheless, by definition coercive. By contrast, the source, and symbol, of Christian authority is the word. This is grounded in the authority that is vested in Christ, the word of God, who himself renounces violence as a means of advancing the kingdom.[19] Both St Paul and the author of Revelation similarly play with the sword/word duality[20] as a means of underlining this point.

Of course, just as the sword can be used unjustly, the word can be used deceitfully, corruptly or violently.[21] Speech can be abused. Nevertheless, the word is, in principle, a weapon of persuasion rather than coercion, and it is the word, rather than the sword, which is to be deployed in determining religious loyalties.

It is this conviction that comes into play when determining the role of the state in securing religious, rather than just Christian, freedom. To coerce people towards Christianity is just as unacceptable as it is to coerce them away from it. Neither lies within the state's proper remit. Christian freedom means enabling people to be secure in a position whereby they can make up their mind on key religious claims without experiencing or fearing coercion.[22]

The point here is not to attempt to create that most chimerical of beasts, the neutral state,[23] but rather to recognise that the principles of wider religious freedom are inherent within Christian thought. Put another way, if we are to adopt an authentically Christian approach to religious freedom, it must be one that is prepared to fight for the right to practice and manifest other religious commitments.

> *An authentically Christian approach to religious freedom must be one that is prepared to fight for the right to practice and manifest other religious commitments.*

This means, with reference to the first principle above, securing the right of religious minorities to worship with the same liberty as a Christian majority would. It also means, in reference to the second principle above, securing the right of such minorities to manifest their religious commitments, because a state that permitted worship (narrowly conceived) but prohibited all, more material manifestations of that worship (such as social service, family life, economic activity, clothing, jewellery, periods of festival, etc.) could legitimately be seen to be practising a form of subtle coercion.

As a coda to this point, it is worth noting that this is one of the functions of the Church of England, at least in the mind of its present governor, the Queen, who observed in a speech at Lambeth Palace in 2012 that the role of the established Church ("occasionally misunderstood and…commonly under-appreciated") is "not to defend Anglicanism to the exclusion of other religions" but "to protect the free practice of all faiths in this country."[24]

1.4 associational rights, beyond those of religious communities, are legitimate

Just as the first two principles taken alone could be construed as placing undue emphasis on Christian freedoms, the first three, taken in isolation, might be seen as placing undue emphasis on religious freedom, inviting the justifiable question, do *religious* commitments automatically have priority over all others? This is where we move from conceptions of and commitments to narrowly-understood religious liberty, to other forms of freedom, which are inherent, if sometimes overlooked, in Christian thought.

When asked which was the greatest commandment, Jesus replied with not one, but two: in St Matthew's version, "Love the Lord your God with all your heart and with all your soul and with all your mind," and "Love your neighbour as yourself."[25] Although clear that the first of these took precedence, his deliberate bracketing of two great commandments, and his comment that the second "is like" the first, are instructive. Human identity and flourishing is grounded in love of one another, as well as of God. In the words of John Paul II's encyclical *Mulieris Dignitatem*, "to be human means to be called to interpersonal communion."[26]

That communion is not narrowly 'religious'. Put another way, love of neighbour may be a moral duty but it is not confined to what goes on in church. This is evident from the Torah, from which Jesus was quoting. This outlines a large number of laws which cover Israel's 'corporate' life as much as the lives of individuals. Over and beyond the explicitly ritual commands, there is legislation concerning governance, legal procedure, economic and environmental practice, and the treatment of immigrants and 'asylum seekers', as well as personal, sexual, family, and community ethics. The objective of this was to demonstrate through the whole community's life – political, legal, economic, environmental, personal, and spiritual – what it was to live with God as sovereign, in order to be an example to surrounding peoples.

The early church was born into rather different circumstances, unable to constitute itself in the way Israel had done. However, it possessed the same DNA and from its earliest moments there are signs that not only was the church to act as a 'living' corporate body within society, but that its activities were not simply narrowly 'religious'. The book of Acts reports how the first believers sold property and possessions and distributed the proceeds to those in need,[27] as well as healing those who were sick and tormented.[28] There was also an early division of such labour, as different groups felt they were being overlooked in the sharing of food, a theme on which St Paul picked up. The church, he explained to his audiences, should operate as a body whose different constituents each had distinct but valuable functions. These were both responsibilities and gifts, various in their purpose, complementary in their merits, equal in worth, but ultimately belonging and bound together under Christ and in love.[29]

> Human identity and flourishing is grounded in love of one another, as well as of God.

In the fullness of time, this became an extraordinarily broad and deep concern with human welfare, especially of the peripheral, in the ancient world. Early Christian teaching placed charity at the centre of spiritual life as no pagan cult had done, raising the care of widows, orphans, the sick, the imprisoned, and the poor to the status of spiritual obligation. It was something which pagans themselves recognised with envy, as evidenced by the oft-quoted words of the last pagan emperor, Julian the Apostate: "it is disgraceful that no Jew is a beggar and the impious Galileans support our poor in addition to their own".[30]

In addition to this, the early church maintained Israel's high opinion of work (an opinion that was not shared in the Greek culture of the ancient near east). Not only did Paul regularly refer to his companions as "co-workers", but he also used the term in a non-metaphorical sense, to describe not only his own industry[31] but also those of fellow Christians. He reserved harsh words for those who, it seems, were free-loading in Thessalonica,[32] whilst, in a more positive register, he recognised in productive employment a redemptive quality, saying to the church in Ephesus that "anyone who has been stealing must steal no longer, but must work, doing something useful with their own hands, that they may have something to share with those in need."[33]

In addition to these views on charity and on work, the activity of government is also legitimated in the Christian scriptures even, crucially, when that government is not exercised by Christians. The New Testament authors had a high opinion of governing, counselling submission to those in authority but also, in several key passages, outlining that not only were those in authority under (the) authority (of Christ) themselves, but that their legitimacy was contingent on the exercise of justice, "punish[ing] those who do wrong and…commend[ing] those who do right," so that "we may live peaceful and quiet lives".[34]

All this is a way of illustrating how Christian scripture and tradition provide a firm basis for the significance and dignity of associational activity in a range of forms that far exceeds the narrowly religious. Whether that is in teaching, healing, serving, working, trading or governing – much of which we would now term as characteristic of civil society – such corporate activity is legitimate, constructive and humanising. Pope Benedict XVI wrote in *Caritas in Veritate* that "it is not by isolation that man [sic] establishes his worth, but by placing himself in relation with others and with God. Hence these relations take on fundamental importance."[35] These "relations" included the formalised and structured ones that naturally populate any society. Recognising the rights and responsibilities of these forms of association is also an important element in navigating the various claims pertaining to religious freedom.

This recognition can be seen in the idea of 'sphere sovereignty', a doctrine derived from Reformed theology and associated with the Dutch theologian and statesman Abraham Kuyper. This argues that since sovereignty belongs to God alone, earthly institutions derive their 'sovereignty' – meaning, in effect, their authority and purpose – from God and his created order, rather than from one another. In other words, families, schools, business, the arts, science and so forth are intrinsically legitimate institutions and activities and do not need the permission of one another, or the state, to exist and operate. So long as their operation pays attention to God's sovereignty, and the limitations that places on their rights and functions, this principle is sound.[36]

Being made up of sinful people, the institutions in question often don't understand, recognise or obey those limits, and have a tendency to overstep their proper function. Accordingly, this principle needs to be held in tension with the others outlined here. Nevertheless, that recognised, the legitimacy – indeed, the social significance – of associational activity is an important factor among the principles of religious freedom, providing as it does a corrective to overly authoritarian government, and overly individualised human rights.

1.5 the family has its own rights but is not sacred or inviolable

The family is unquestionably one of the social institutions that is 'sovereign' within its own sphere, and is thus covered by the previous principle. However, given the manner in which secularist groups repeatedly home in on the rights of parents to brings up their children in their faith, not to mention the manner in which strands of Christian thinking have turned honouring the family into a shibboleth of orthodoxy, it is worth focusing specifically, if briefly, on the family itself.

There is a clichéd view in which the family is somehow seen as synonymous with Christianity, in which hearth and home become the domestic mirror image of throne and altar. In actual fact, specific New Testament teaching on the family is spare, and the only document to place a singular emphasis on it is 1 Timothy, in which the author advises that he who wishes to be an overseer "must manage his own family well and see that his children obey him, and he must do so in a manner worthy of full respect", reasoning that "if anyone does not know how to manage his own family, how can he take care of God's church?"[37] The family, he later writes, should serve as the primary locus of care, children putting their religion "into practice" by caring for parents and grandparents.[38]

Against this, Jesus himself relativised family bonds in a highly provocative way. Early on in his ministry, when his mother and brothers came looking for him as he was preaching, Jesus asked rhetorically, "Who are my mother and my brothers?", before redefining the terms: "Whoever does God's will is my brother and sister and mother."[39] It was not an isolated incident. Later on, in Luke's gospel, he said to a man who offered to follow him but first wished to bury his father, "let the dead bury their own dead". To another, who asked if he might first go back and say goodbye to his family, Jesus said "no one who puts a hand to the plough and looks back is fit for service in the kingdom of God."[40] These stories retain the power to shock, even today. It is hard to grasp quite how offensive they were at the time.

These two sentiments seem to be in tension with one another, but there is a third factor which is relevant, namely the extent to which 'family', and attendant terms, is used as a metaphor for the mutuality, and selfless and sustained care and responsibility, that was supposed to mark the early church communities.

Paul speaks of doing good to all people, "especially to those who belong to the family of believers".[41] Peter exhorts his audience to "love the family of believers".[42] James addresses his "brothers and sisters", meaning not his blood-relations but those believers who are part of God's family. Even Jesus' abrasive redefinition of the family in Mark 3/Matthew 12/Luke 8 only retains its power if family bonds are seen as being important in the first place. Were they otherwise, calling those who do God's will "my brother and sister and mother" would not be an act of approval but one of indifference.

This metaphor, or series of metaphors, extends beyond the ecclesial community, to more fundamental images: God as father, believers as his children, church as Christ's bride. These are the ideas and metaphors by means of which we are to grasp the relational structures of reality and redemption; their absolute centrality to the gospel speaks of the significance rather than the insignificance of 'family'.

The third factor helps us understand the apparent tension within the first two. The choice of the metaphor of 'family', in its various permutations, to describe God's love of and attitude towards his people, and theirs towards one another, simultaneously sanctifies the family, by suggesting there is no earthly network of relationships that better captures God's love and care, and undermines it, by placing God's familial commitments over and above earthly ones.

How that maps onto a principle on which we can draw when navigating the field of religion and law is not straightforward. On the one hand, it underpins the teaching that the family is its own authority and does not need the permission of the state to exist and operate. In the words of Catholic Social Teaching, "the Church considers the family as the first natural society, with underived rights that are proper to it, and places it at the centre of social life."[43] Like other forms of associational activity discussed above, but more so, the family has its own inherent life and dignity.

On the other hand, the family is not unchallengeably sacred or imbued with an authority before which all other bodies in society must bow. Families can be abusive, or dehumanising, and they stand in judgement just as do all other relational structures that humans form. It is possible to 'interfere' with them without doing them a violence or injustice.

That noted, it is important to recognise that the fact that the judgement under which the family is placed in the gospels is the call of Christ strongly suggests that the bar for interference is set very high. Interfering with family life should not be undertaken casually or without very good reason, but it may be necessary and legitimate nonetheless.

1.6 human dignity, as expressed in rights, is an authentic Christian principle

If any one conflict epitomises the tensions surrounding religious freedom, it is the *alleged* conflict between human rights and religious rights. The emphasis is important. Some people do apparently see human rights as a counter-balance to religious rights, a line drawn around the human that cannot be crossed no matter what religious rights are circumscribed in the process.

That recognised, contrary to such impressions, human and religious rights do not necessarily stand in opposition to one another, whether legally (religious rights are also human rights), philosophically (human rights, as distinct from any purportedly adhering to other sentient creatures, depend on some concept of humanity and, in particular, human dignity), or historically (the idea of human rights owes something – how much is debated

– to the idea that all humans are made in the image of God and possessed of an inherent and inalienable dignity).

Although some have disputed the directness of the link between Christianity and human rights,[44] the connection between such rights and the idea that humans are made 'in the image of God'[45] (and then remade in the image of Christ[46]) and thus are possessed of an inviolable worth, is a strong one.[47] The underlying idea of human rights, whatever quibbles there many be about the precise realisation of that idea, is emphatically not foreign to Christian thought. In the words of Catholic Social Teaching, "the movement towards the identification and proclamation of human rights is one of the most significant attempts to respond effectively to the inescapable demands of human dignity."[48]

A conviction of human worth underpinned the extension of the idea of personhood, a limited, legal concept in the ancient world, to those who were on the periphery of society, up to and even including slaves, many of whom were otherwise non-persons in society.[49] Of course, Christian practice has often fallen short of this ideal, although perhaps not as short as some imagine. Nevertheless, the point remains that the idea of human rights is not only not antithetical to Christianity, but is wholly consonant with a tradition that recognises an inherent and inalienable dignity within the human.

The key question is what constitutes an infringement of human dignity or rights sufficient to demand curtailment of religious liberty. It is easy to see where the line is definitively crossed. On the one hand, for example, there is general – though by no means unanimous – acceptance, within the UK, of the Jewish practice of infant male circumcision.[50] On the other, there is general – though again not unanimous – agreement that female genital mutilation is unacceptable.

However, when one gets to more liminal issues, such as time off, the right to serve the public through organisations ordered according to religious principles, to wear or carry religious accessories, the understanding and regulation of gender roles and sexual conduct, clothing regulations, or the manner in which animals are killed, then different people will have (strongly) different views based on different conceptions of the good. The extent to which such practices are permitted or prohibited will depend, in part, on the extent to which they are indeed intrinsic to the religious traditions in question (cf. principles 2 and 3 above, and also part 2 of this essay) but they will also reflect the extent to which they genuinely infringe human dignity.

Because of this, and the growing sense that genuine human goods are so varied and incommensurable, and that therefore the differences in opinion are not amenable to rational calculation or resolution, there has been a tendency to cut through the Gordian knot with a straightforward appeal to agency and consent: if someone willingly selects something for themselves, whether clothing or practice, it cannot, by definition constitute an infringement of their rights. Conversely, if they don't choose it for themselves, it cannot be legitimate. Choice is not simply necessary but sufficient as a way of dissolving the challenges posed by human rights, providing no-one else is 'harmed' by the practice chosen.

Putting aside the difficulties there are in calculating harm, this resort to agency and consent alone is hard to reconcile with a Christian understanding of human rights (or dignity), which are not subjective and infinitely malleable, but predicated on God's equal love of all persons. Humans cannot be each other's objects but nor are they solely subjects with no worth beyond their capacity to act freely.

> *We cannot short-cut all such difficult arguments by mere appeal to personal choice. "I want" is not a moral argument.*

According to this view, human dignity is indeed tied up with the capacity to exercise moral will, but it is not synonymous with it, and the right to choose does not automatically take precedence over that which is chosen, even when the harm principle does not come into play. We cannot short-cut all such difficult arguments by mere appeal to personal choice. "I want" is not a moral argument.

The key point within this principle is not, however, its considerable complexity (that is merely a warning of what we should expect when employing ideas of human rights). Rather, it is that the principle of inherent, equal and inalienable human dignity is central to the Christian tradition, and foundational to the idea of human rights. Whatever nervousness there is in many quarters about the extent and realisation of human rights, religious and human rights are not inherently antithetical. That does not mean there are no tensions between the two categories, or that religious rights do not need to negotiate and compromise with other human rights. Rather, it means that this process of negotiation and compromise is not inherently antagonistic, nor an inherently foreign, 'secular' imposition upon the Christian legal and ethical framework.

1.7 equality does not mean sameness or necessitate identical treatment

Lord Bingham once wrote that St Paul "committed himself repeatedly and unambiguously to what must at the time have been an astonishing, and what remains an impressive and remarkable, belief in the principle of non-discrimination", quoting various of Paul's letters in support.[51] This is correct, although it is worth noting that Paul's justification for this "non-discrimination" (a somewhat anachronistic term) is repeatedly located in the activity of

God. In other words, the equal and inalienable worth that inheres within persons does so on account of divine love rather than any earthly status.

The Christian idea of equality is grounded in the fact that, in Nicholas Wolterstorff's words, "God loves equally and permanently each and every creature who bears the *imago dei*… bearing that property gives to each human being who bears it the worth in which natural human rights inhere". It is not grounded in the fact that all people have equal merits or, still less, are all the same. According to the Christian tradition it is not who or how good you are that justifies your equal treatment as a person of worth. Rather, "what I recognize in recognizing the dignity of the other is that they have a standing before God, which is, of its nature, invulnerable to the success or failure of any other relationship or any situation in the contingent world."[52]

A concomitant fact in all this is that humans, and the groups they form, can be different and, by dint of their difference, treated differently without necessarily infringing their inherent and equal dignity. Human diversity is not obliterated by the recognition or even realisation of that equality. Equality does not mean sameness.

Equality does not mean sameness.

This is seen in various vignettes within the biblical narrative, such as Pentecost, in which the same message is broadcast in languages accommodated to people's cultures, or Revelation, where the eschatological community is repeatedly identified by its quintessential and distinguishing characteristics of "tribe, language, people, and nation."[53] Equal access to the message or the throne of God is not predicated on people speaking the same language or possessing the same ethnic or national characteristics.

The same idea is more substantially seen in Paul's teaching on the body of Christ. Here the bond is of mutual service and belonging – "if one part suffers, every part suffers with it; if one part is honoured, every part rejoices with it." Importantly, however, these *different* roles are treated as having *equal* worth and dignity. "Those parts of the body that seem to be weaker are indispensable, and the parts that we think are less honourable we treat with special honour."[54] The controlling idea is one of unity based on reciprocity and mutual respect because – not in spite – of difference.[55]

A commitment to equality, therefore, is not necessarily a commitment to sameness in the sense of identical treatment. Different people and different organisations can in certain situations be treated differently without infringing their equality. We can legitimately 'discriminate' – using the term neutrally to mean discern and evaluate on relevant grounds rather than pejoratively to mean decide according to prejudice.

This is not, in fact, as controversial as it may seem. All judges use their discretion when sentencing, taking into account, for example, the circumstances of the crime and its perpetrator when passing judgment. The same crime may be treated differently depending, say, on the level of contextual provocation, humiliation, and abuse. Wives who take their husbands' lives are not all to be punished in the same way. Justice and true equality can require unequal treatment.

The same principles apply when dealing with religious groups and religious freedom. Just because it is easy to lump very different groups and activities under the category of 'religious' (a blurred and somewhat artificial term) that does not mean they should all be treated in precisely the same way. Categories can be unhelpfully broad and vague ('religion' is) and it is entirely within a proper understanding of equal standing under a common law to accommodate context into political, legal and ethical decisions.

This is – or, rather, is often seen as – an unjust and inflammatory approach. After the then BBC Director General, Mark Thompson, delivered the inaugural Theos Annual Lecture in 2008 he was asked whether recent reports that the BBC treated Islam and Christianity differently were right. Without saying 'yes' outright, he explained why the BBC *might* treat different religions differently. There was a minor outcry, culminating in a nasty *Daily Star* front page two days later. When, a few years later, the Archbishop of Canterbury, Rowan Williams, delivered a lecture on the relationship between Islamic and English law, albeit heavily qualified and examined, he was drawing on similar logic, and there was an even bigger outrage.

Quoting these two examples is not to offer unqualified approval for either view. One could mount arguments for sameness of treatment in both instances. Indeed, if a category is coherent enough to be intelligible – and 'religion' for all its problems is intelligible – it is fair to assume that equality of treatment should be the normative position for all that falls within that category. 'Treat similar things similarly' is a good rule of thumb. Christianity and Islam (and Buddhism, and Taoism…), in as far as they are comparable religions, should enjoy equal and same treatment under a common law.

Nevertheless, this is a normative position from which departure, on the basis of legitimate distinctions, may be legitimate. It may be that differences in theological, or socio-economic, or demographic, or historical, or cultural criteria mean that different religions may be treated in different ways. This is not an alien idea. Indeed, it is already assumed in the particular role of Christianity in certain national affairs, say in parliamentary business or the Coronation, or when courts take into account the different duties inherent in different religions. Because Christianity stands, historically and culturally, in a very different place to other religions, it may be right for it to be treated differently, without infringing fundamental tenets of equality (this specific question is picked up in the second part of this essay).

The key point, then, is that according to Christian thought, human equality is grounded in God's ineradicable love, but does not obliterate particularity. Different things may legitimately be treated differently if there are sufficient and relevant grounds for doing so.

conclusion

The first half of this essay has sought to set out a number of principles by means of which Christians might negotiate the increasingly fraught debate around religious freedom in contemporary Britain. In summary these are:

1. Human nature finds its fulfilment in communion with God, and the state is under obligation to recognise and respect this inherent 'spiritual' nature.

2. That 'spiritual' communion has an irreducible materiality to it. Freedom of religion cannot be reduced to freedom of belief or freedom to conduct religious services without doing violence to the spiritual relationship that is at its heart.

3. Religious commitment should be determined by persuasion rather than coercion. This means that the first two principles need to be made available for all religions. Christians should be prepared to fight for the right to practice and manifest other religious commitments, or indeed the right to hold none.

4. Christian scripture and tradition provide a firm basis for the significance and dignity of associational activity, such as in teaching, healing, serving, working, trading, or governing, and for conducting such activities from authentically religious (as opposed to feigned secular) motivations. These activities, familiar to us under the rubric of 'civil society' have their own rights and responsibilities towards the wider public good, which demand consideration alongside claims of more narrowly-conceived 'religious freedom'.

5. The family has its own authority and duties and does not need the permission of the state to exist and operate. However, it, like all other bodies in society, is under authority and judgment, and this means that the state may intervene when there is sufficient cause without transgressing that authority.

6. The principle of inherent, equal and inalienable human dignity is central to the Christian tradition, and foundational to the idea of human rights. Whatever nervousness there is in many quarters about the extent and realisation of human

rights, religious and human rights are not inherently antithetical. Counter-balancing religious rights with other human rights is not a foreign, 'secular' imposition upon the Christian legal and ethic framework but part of that framework itself.

7.   Human diversity is not obliterated by the recognition or even realisation of equality. Humans, and the groups they form, are different and, by dint of their difference, may be treated differently without necessarily infringing their inherent dignity.

These principles are not incontestable and nor are they exhaustive. They do not offer a clear cut answer that will solve legal and religious disputes that are often, of their very nature, insoluble. Claims of freedom and equality are always in tension, at least as soon as they rise above minimal levels. Freedom of conscience or belief might be reasonably easy to reconcile with abstract ideas of human equality, but as soon as the former becomes freedom to live according to conscience or belief, or the latter becomes a more concrete endeavour to realise that equality materially or socially, tensions arise.

There is nothing suspect in this. It is, rather, a natural concomitant of the human condition, particularly as lived in a culturally, socially, religiously, and ideologically diverse society such as ours. We must simply be alert to this complexity, and be prepared to enter into negotiation, something that is made easier by ascertaining principles for negotiation in the first place.

It may be that, even when such principles have been outlined, the consequence of their deployment is to leave us with the status quo, or something very like it. For all that some people like to claim (or imply) that the courts are stacked against Christianity, Britain has nothing like the egregious examples of atheistic culture with which this essay began, and for the most part functions well. It may be that the biblical and theological principles with which we start point us back towards where we are.

> *If religious identity and values are viewed through a secular prism, they are in danger of being seen and treated as quasi-secular identities and values.*

That recognised, however, although many of the principles outlined above are undoubtedly reflected in our present arrangements, there seems likely to be subtle but important differences of emphases.

Living on the other side of the totalitarian horrors of the 20th century, we are sometimes in danger of unquestioningly genuflecting before the altar of human rights, principle six above assuming the centre of gravity, around which the others move. As already stressed, the Christian tradition has no necessary problem with human rights. The idea of human dignity is central to its teachings. However, human dignity being irreducibly relational in nature, at least according to Christian thought, the principle of human rights – particularly individualised human rights – is not necessarily the centre of gravity but rather assumes a position alongside others – a fact which invites an obvious but problematic question: which of these principles should sit at the hub of the wheel?

This is a difficult question. On the one hand, it is hard to see how the principles outlined above can be established into a rigid and permanent hierarchy (to change metaphors). Even if some of the principles – such as those pertaining to religious freedom or that pertaining to human rights – were deemed generally of a higher order than others (such as that pertaining to associational freedom), it is hard to see how one must always and inflexibly be 'superior' to the others.

Historical examples of intolerable religious practice (such as slavery or human sacrifice) show how, in extreme cases, it is not only acceptable but mandatory to interfere with religious practice, however sincerely it may be held. Conversely, were it the case that 'human rights' (narrowly conceived) were always elevated above 'religious rights' (narrowly conceived), the latter would become close to worthless – a playing card that could always and everywhere be trumped.

If the principles above differ from mainstream liberal thought in any specific way, it is perhaps in the recognition that there is a danger in a semi-secularised society such as our own, much of which is unaware of or indifferent to the contours of organised religious faith, that insufficient attention is paid to the principles of religious conscience, worship, and practice. Put another way, if religious identity and values are viewed through a secular prism, they are in danger of being seen and treated as quasi-secular identities and values, the inherent multi-dimensionality of a life lived in reference to the divine being flattened out into wholly temporal or secular categories. To borrow Julian Rivers' neologism, it leads to the "recreationalisation" of religion, turning it into "another hobby". In this understanding,

> the law need make no space for the idea that there might actually be a God, who might really be calling people into relationship with himself, who might make real demands on his worshippers. Religion thus acquires all the moral weight of stampcollecting or train-spotting.[56]

If there is any obvious difference between where these Christian principles might direct us, compared with where other, more nakedly secular ones might, it lies here. Religious rights do not automatically trump all other rights. Neither they nor any other rights comprise a 'get out of jail free' card. However, religious rights are, certainly according to Christian thought, central to who we are as people and require recognition accordingly.

It is no accident that the first freedom to be pursued in Britain was, in effect, religious freedom, as various Protestant groups sought to worship in their own particular ways in the early seventeenth century. This is consonant with the Christian idea that the human good is bound up with relationship with God. But it is also more than simply self-serving, for it is on the basis that humans are largely free to orient themselves as they wish with regard to the big existential questions of purpose, identity, destiny and the good, that other earthly freedoms are often constructed. The freedom to speak, to assemble, to campaign and to co-operate is hard to sustain if the ultimate reasons for that speech, assembly and co-operation are denied. In the words of Canadian Minister John Baird at the Religious Liberty Dinner in 2012 "societies that protect religious freedom are more likely to protect other fundamental freedoms."[57]

> The freedom to speak, to assemble, to campaign and to co-operate is hard to sustain if the ultimate reasons for that speech, assembly and co-operation are denied. Societies that protect religious freedom are more likely to protect other fundamental freedoms.

This, then, is the co-ordinating idea that may be used when deploying the principles outlined above: not that religious freedom must be honoured above all other principles but that, in the fluid balance of principles in which no one principle serves as an immutable centre of gravity for all the others, a proper recognition of the intrinsic nature of religious liberty must be allowed to take its full and proper place in discussions. What this might look like is the subject of the second part of this essay.

chapter 1 references

1   See Yiwu Liao, *God is Red: The Secret Story of How Christianity Survived and Flourished in Communist China* (HarperOne, 2011).

2   Article 66: "all citizens who have reached the age of 17 shall have the right to vote and the right to be elected, irrespective of…religious belief"; Article 68: "citizens shall have freedom of religion… guaranteed by permitting the construction of religious buildings and the holding of religious ceremonies," before adding that "religion shall not be used in bringing in outside forces or in harming the state and social order."

3   See Barbara Demick, *Nothing to Envy: Real Lives in North Korea* (Granta Books, 2010); Janet Chismar, 'Against All Odds: Faith Flourishes Quietly in North Korea', *Religion Today*," 25 October 2001; Doug Struck, 'Keeping the Faith, Underground', *Washington Post*, 10 April 2001.

4   Not all legal analyses do this. Rex Ahdar and Ian Leigh, in their book *Religious Freedom in the Liberal State* (Oxford: OUP, 2005; rev. 2013) outline eight Christian principles for religious freedom, namely (1) the principle of voluntariness (faith demands a free response); (2) the Christological injunction (the Son of God compelled no-one to follow him); (3) the persecution injunction (persecution in the name of God is an offence to him); (4) the fallibility principle (humans cannot judge others, and especially not others' faith, infallibly so shouldn't try); (5) the eschatological or providential principle (truth and goodness will work out of God's principles naturally and eventually); (6) the ecumenical or universal principle (God will speak in and through all manner of unexpected places which shouldn't be silenced); (7) the principle of unrestrained conscience (the need to respect the demands of conscience); and (8) the dual authority principles (there are strict limitations on the state's right to interfere with personal spiritual matters). See pp. 23-50.

5   Jeremy Waldron, 'Legislation and Moral Neutrality' in *Liberal Rights: Collected Papers 1981-1991* (Cambridge, 1993) p. 153; emphases original.

6   Which provides that (1) "Everyone has the right to freedom of thought, conscience and religion; this right includes freedom to change his religion or belief, and freedom, either alone or in community with others and in public or private, to manifest his religion or belief, in worship, teaching, practice and observance", and (2) "Freedom to manifest one's religion or beliefs shall be subject only to such limitations as are prescribed by law and are necessary in a democratic society in the interests of public safety, for the protection of public order, health or morals, or the protection of the rights and freedoms of others".

7   Specifically: age, disability, gender reassignment, marriage and civil partnership, race, sex, and sexual orientation.

8   Russell Sandberg, *Religion and Law* (Cambridge: Cambridge University Press, 2011), p. 195.

9   Ibid, pp. 193-94.

10 Ibid, p. 35.

11 Jonathan Sumption, 'The Limits of Law', the 27th Sultan Azlan Shah Lecture, Kuala Lumpur, 20th November 2013; http://www.supremecourt.gov.uk/docs/speech-131120.pdf

12 It is worth noting that Sumption's objection here has little to do with the content of the European decisions – "Personally, if I may be allowed to speak as a citizen, I think that most of the values which underlie judicial decisions on human rights, both at Strasbourg and in the domestic courts of the United Kingdom, are wholly admirable" – but rather the fact of them – "But it does not follow that I am at liberty to impose them on a majority of my fellow-citizens without any democratic process." His concern, a wholly legitimate one in my view, is that such European juridification ultimately and badly undermines domestic political sovereignty.

13   Isaiah 66.18: "I…am about to come and gather the people of all nations and languages, and they will come and see my glory."

14   Revelation 21.3-5: "God's dwelling place is now among the people, and he will dwell with them. They will be his people, and God himself will be with them and be their God. 'He will wipe every tear from their eyes. There will be no more death' or mourning or crying or pain, for the old order of things has passed away."

15   Benedict XVI, *Caritas in Veritate, #54. The verse is from* John 17.22.

16   John Zizilous, *Being as Communion: studies in personhood and the church* (Crestwood, N.Y. : St. Vladimir's Seminary Press, 1985).

17   See Nick Spencer, *Neither Private nor Privileged: The Role of Christianity in Britain Today* (London: Theos, 2008).

18   Romans 13.4.

19   See: Matthew 28.18, John 1.1, Matthew 26.52; John 18.11.

20   Ephesians 6.17; Revelation 19.15.

21   cf. James 3.6; Matthew 5.33-37; Matthew 5.22.

22   Some secularists adopt this as an argument for disestablishment or complete separation of church (or religion) and state, such as in America. This, however, is to load the argument with conclusions it cannot (and need not) sustain. It was, after all, self-consciously Christian Victorian England, with its firmly established church, that slowly unwound the legislation which saw the promotion of Christianity as part of the state's duty. Separation of church and state is one option, but it is entirely possible to have an established religion without contravening the principle of 'persuasion not coercion' in religious matters.

23   Or even the religiously-neutral state: just as states cannot be indifferent to moral issues, nor are they indifferent to religious ones, the US being the exception that proves the rule.

24   http://www.royal.gov.uk/LatestNewsandDiary/Speechesandarticles/2012/ TheQueensspeechatLambethpalace15February2012.aspx

25   Matthew 22.37-39.

26   John Paul II, *Mulieris Dignitatem*, #7.

27   Acts 2.45; Acts 4.35.

28   Acts 5.16.

29   Romans 12.3-8; 1 Corinthians 12.12-31; Ephesians 4.11-13.

30   Letter to Arsacius, quoted in D. Brendan Nagle (ed.) *The Roman World: Sources And Interpretation* (ed.) D. Brendan Nagle (Pearson/Prentice Hall, 2005), p. 269.

31   1 Corinthians 9.6.

32   2 Thessalonians 3.10.

33   Ephesians 4.28.

34   Romans 13.1-7; 1 Peter 2.13; 1 Timothy 2.2.

35   *Caritas in Veritate*, #53.

36   See Peter Heslam, *Creating a Christian Worldview: Abraham Kuyper's Lectures on Calvinism* (William B Eerdmans Publishing, 1998).

37   1 Timothy 3.4-5.

38   1 Timothy 5.4.

39   Mark 3.31-35.

40   Luke 9.57-62.

41   Galatians 6.10.

42   1 Peter 2.17.

43   Pontifical Council for Justice and Peace, *Compendium of the Social Doctrine of the Church* (Continuum, 2004), sect. 211.

44   See, for example, Lord Bingham of Cornhill, 'Endowed by their Creator?', in *Ecclesiastical Law Journal*, Volume 8, Issue 37, July 2005, pp 173-185.

45   Genesis 1.26-27; Psalm 8.

46   2 Corinthians 3.18, Colossians 3.10.

47   See Nicholas Wolterstorff, *Justice: Rights and Wrongs* (Princeton University Press, 2010); Julian Rivers, 'The Nature and Role of Government in the Bible', in Nick Spencer and Jonathan Chaplin (eds.), *God and Government*, (SPCK, 2009); Roger Ruston, *Human Rights and the Image of God* (SCM, 2004); Christopher Marshall, *Crowned with Glory and Honor: Human Rights in the Biblical Tradition* (Herald Press, 2002).

48   *Compendium of the Social Doctrine*, sect. 152.

49   When church father Gregory of Nyssa fulminated against the institution of slavery itself in the later fourth century, denouncing Christians for daring to imagine they could own another human being when such a right belonged to God alone, he was voicing an opinion that was extreme within the church but completely unheard of beyond it.

50   This is a much more contentious issue in Germany where a court in Cologne banned the practice in 2012, precipitating a heated public debate and a parliamentary bill to keep the practice legal. See, http://www.dw.de/circumcision-remains-legal-in-germany/a-16399336

51   Romans 2.11; 10.12; 1 Corinthians 12.13; Galatians 3,28; Colossians. 3.11. Bingham of Cornhill, 'Endowed by their Creator', op. cit. pp. 179-80.

52   Rowan Williams, *Faith in the Public Square* (London: Bloomsbury, 2012), p. 171.

53   Acts 2.1-13; Revelation 5.9, 7.9.

54   Romans 12.3-8; 1 Corinthians 12.12-31.

55   2 Corinthians 8.1-15.

56   Quoted in Matthew Gibson, 'The God "Dilution"? Religion, discrimation and the case for reasonable accommodation', *The Cambridge Law Journal*, 72 (2013), pp. 578-616.

57   http://www.international.gc.ca/media/aff/speeches-discours/2012/05/24a.aspx

questions of religious freedom

2.1 does true religious freedom necessitate disestablishment?

The establishment of the Church is a particular target for secularist groups. "One of the primary, long-terms aims of the National Secular Society is the disestablishment of the Church of England".[1] "The Anglican Church is still the state church of England. We", the British Humanist Association writes, "wish to see it disestablished."[2]

Historically, it is easy to see why this is such an issue for such secularist organisations. All major European countries sustained some form of ecclesiastical establishment up until the 20th century, and in many instances that establishment entailed severely infringing religious freedom and even the creation of a *de facto* two-tier citizenry, with those of different or no religious faith relegated to the lower rank. Were this to be the case today, it would obviously contradict some of the principles outlined in part one and therefore be unsustainable. The complication – and it is a major one – lies in the fact that establishment is not one thing, and the automatic association of establishment with inequality, unfairness, or infringed rights is questionable.

Broadly speaking, jurists distinguish between three models of church-state relations: unity, separation, and hybrid. Unity systems are those where there are close, constitutional links between the state and one (or more) religious institution. Often styled 'state', 'national', 'established', or 'folk' churches, these enjoy certain constitutional privileges, on the one hand, and certain administrative responsibilities on the other. Such systems exist, in different forms, in England, Scotland, Denmark, Greece, Finland and Malta.

Separation systems are at the other end of the spectrum, where state and church are formally separate and there is often some kind of constitutional barrier that forbids the state's financial or legal support of any particular religious institution. Often termed secular, these systems vary but can be recognised in France, Australia and, most famously, America.

Hybrid systems, also sometimes known as 'cooperationist' or 'concordatarian' systems, have a formal separation of church and state, but are also marked by various agreements, treaties and concordats between the church and particular religious groups, which recognise certain mutual rights and responsibilities. Such an arrangement can be found in Spain, Italy, Germany, Belgium, Austria, Hungary, Portugal and the Baltic States.

This tri-partite division is anything but watertight or clearly graduated. A secular system, such as France, can interfere in religious affairs both negatively (banning headscarves and other "conspicuous" religious symbols in schools, and all forms of face covering in public) and positively (paying for the upkeep of churches built before 1905). A hybrid system, such as Spain or Germany, may offer more financial or practical support of a church, such as the funding of exclusively Catholic chaplains in schools, hospitals and prisons, or the state-collection of taxes from church members, than an established system such as in England.

This is not the place to tease apart the various different permutations inherent in establishment, so much as to point out that "the *de jure* relationship between religion and state may not necessarily coincide with the *de facto* connection."[3] In short, we blunt our discussion of the presenting question if we treat establishment as an obvious, homogenous and always problematic thing.

The question of whether principled religious freedom necessitates disestablishment depends, in large measure, on what it is being disestablished; on what, in the jargon, are the "incidents of establishment". These differ in England and Scotland, and even Wales, where the church was formally disestablished in 1920. Although the precise details are complex,[4] the principal incidents are well known.

In England, the monarch is the Supreme Governor of the Church of England, though not necessarily a member of that church (George I was a Lutheran, for example), and must be in communion with the Church. Twenty-six Anglican bishops sit in House of Lords by right, as Lords Spiritual, until they retire, reading prayers at the start of the parliamentary day. Members of other religious traditions may be appointed to Lords under the Life Peerages Act 1958, but do not sit *by right* or as Lords Spiritual.

Along with these rights, come certain restrictions and responsibilities. The monarch is the "Supreme Governor" of the established church thereby subjecting church rules to Parliamentary oversight. Church of England law requires Royal Assent, thereby receiving the status of State law. Ecclesiastical courts and their jurisprudence are part of the law of the land, meaning that their decisions are subject to judicial review by the High Court. Provisions are found in the Civil Partnership Act 2004, which allow that government ministers may amend or repeal "church legislation", which, in the words of Mark Hill, "amounts to a curtailment of autonomy on the part of the Church of England, albeit partial, with a specificity of purpose, and reliant upon benign and consensual exercise by the Government".[5] In terms of responsibilities, the Church of England has a formalised public ministry. This means, among other things, that people resident in parishes cannot be excluded from public worship there, and parishioners, and now those with "qualifying connections", enjoy the legal right to be married in the parish church.

Scotland has a 'softer' form of establishment, whereby the monarch swears an oath to protect the Church (of which s/he is not governor but simply a member), and the Church's independence in "matters spiritual" is formally recognised. The Church in Wales, disestablished since 1920, has no bishops sitting in the Lords, no law that is recognised as state law, and is free from Crown interference with regard to appointments. In reality, however, it is still "a hybrid of the established and non-established churches", with certain vestiges of establishment remaining.[6] These various incidents of establishment are somewhat different from those in, say, Denmark,[7] Greece,[8] Finland[9] or Malta[10] where the relative rights and restrictions are greater.

> It is not 'secularism' vs. 'establishment' so much as 'do the incidents of a particular establishment enable or infringe religious freedom?'

This variety of forms of establishment, not to mention the variety of secular settlements, may serve to remind us that the question is not whether we should favour an established, hybrid or secular arrangements *per se*, but whether a particular settlement is consonant with the principles of religious freedom. It is not 'secularism' vs. 'establishment' (as if they were self-evident and homogenous categories) so much as 'do the incidents of a particular establishment, or indeed the contours of a particular secular settlement, enable or infringe religious freedom?'

This is the position favoured by European law. The European Union has repeatedly accepted a variety of church-state relations as being part of a contracting state's 'margin of appreciation', the legitimate difference in interpretation of the law among different member states. Mild forms of state preference for one religion over another do not violate the European Convention of Human Rights, on the proviso that that preference does not infringe the religious freedom of those who do not conform to the 'state' Church. Thus, in *Darby v. Sweden*, in which a Finnish citizen of British origin disputed a church tax that was paid to the Swedish authorities as part of his municipal taxation, the court stated that "a State Church system cannot in itself be considered to violate Article 9 of the Convention", before adding the caveat that "a State Church system must, in order to satisfy Article 9, include specific safeguards for the individual's freedom of religion."[11] In short, legal preference for a certain religion is compatible with the freedom of religion "provided that legal preference is not accompanied by distinct civil and legal disabilities for the non-adherents of the official religion."[12]

If this is so, the question becomes a more empirical one. Does establishment (or secularism) entail civil and legal disabilities for those people who differ in their affiliation from the favoured institution or settlement? A generalised answer to this is evidenced by the Democracy Index calculated on a bi-annual basis by the Economic Intelligence Unit. This measures the state of 'electoral processes and pluralism', 'civil liberties', 'the functioning of government', 'political participation' and 'political culture' in 167 countries, placing each into one of four categories: 'full democracies', 'flawed democracies', 'hybrid regimes', and 'authoritarian regimes'.

The results are instructive. Countries like the USA, Japan, Australia and the Netherlands – with thoroughly or predominantly secular settlements – are all categorised as 'full democracies'. But so are Iceland, Denmark, Finland, Switzerland, Germany, Spain and Malta, which boast either 'established' churches or 'cooperationist' settlements. The UK, with two separate established churches, is a low-scoring 'full democracy', coming 16th in the overall list, a level not so much due to its poor record on civil liberties (in which it comes 23rd) as its low levels of political engagement (in which it came 33rd).

Historically, of course, the situation was very different. To be a member of anything other than the established church before about 1830 was to know sustained religious and civil disabilities, and even after that date it was to endure *ad hoc* legal disabilities, until the early 20th century. Some claim that such disabilities exist today, but with the final abolition of the blasphemy laws in 2008, it is hard to see where they lie. The manner in which the National Secular Society threatened legal action against Woking Borough Council for waiving its three pound parking fee for Sunday morning worshippers rather makes this point.[13]

> *Mild forms of state preference for one religion over another do not violate the European Convention of Human Rights.*

The answer to the headline question, therefore, seems to be 'no': true religious freedom does not necessitate disestablishment. However, it is a 'no but…', rather than a straightforward denial. Establishment patently can entail civil and religious disabilities and its continued existence depends on its willingness to avoid them. In the words of one scholar, establishment in England has survived "because the Church of England quickly understood the need to accept religious pluralism and chose to exercise its prerogatives and political power in favour of all religion."[14]

This is clearly an acceptable, indeed desirable condition for many Christians, not least the current monarch who has been uncharacteristically outspoken in her defence of the Church of England on precisely this basis. But it is not acceptable for others, who see it as an improper restriction on the church's mission.

This point clearly invites a sustained discussion of the merits and problems of establishment. Is it an anachronism? An undue privilege? Does it constitute an untenable intrusion of the state into spiritual affairs? Is it a necessary reminder that God rather than state is the ultimate source of political authority? That the state is under moral authority less fickle than public opinion? Does it protect the spiritual lives of all citizens from the secularist tendency to privatise and trivialise them?

Sadly, this is not the place for such a debate, which would demand a full essay in itself. This section is not so much an attempt to rehearse, still less to adjudicate on, the arguments pertaining to establishment, as to offer a way of thinking about religious freedom vis-à-vis establishment, by asking whether the two are compatible. The conclusion is that they are, if certain conditions are met.

A coda with which to close: the more attentive readers will notice that one of the supposed incidents of establishment in England has been largely absent from the discussion, namely the presence of bishops in the House of Lords. This is deliberate. Although this is an incident of establishment in England (though not in Scotland) in as far as the Lords Spiritual exist because of establishment, it is not synonymous with it. It would be possible to remove bishops without disestablishing the church, although to do so would be to remove one of the features that signifies the distinctive relationship between church and state in England, even if it does not technically embody it. The issue of bishops in the Lords is not, therefore, strictly one of establishment but is, rather, tied up with the wider question of what the second chamber is for. The fact that wrangles about the House of Lords' composition are on-going suggest that this is a question on which we are far from decided.

2.2 should religious groups be free to run according to their own rules?

The apparent right of religious groups to organise and operate according to their own rules is often badly misunderstood and, consequently, the source of much public resentment. It is not uncommon to hear the complaint that religious groups are 'exempt from' or 'above' the law that applies 'to the rest of us'. Understandably, this view breeds antagonism.

It is mistaken. Humans are naturally group-forming beings and for groups to be groups – as opposed to aggregations of individuals – they need various rules and regulations to constitute, shape and protect them. Such rules and regulations do not replace the 'normal' laws under which people live, still less excuse them from obeying those normal laws. They are not coercive, in the sense of exercising power over a person against of their will, nor are they compulsory, in the sense of denying people the right of exit. Rather they are binding but on a voluntary basis. Religious groups in the UK (with the exception of the Church of

England) are, in this regard at least, no different to sports clubs, their regulations based on "consensual compact", a private, voluntary agreement, as with any unincorporated association or members club.

Although there is self-evidently nothing sinister in this, there is clearly potential for tension, for a number of reasons. First, groups (because comprised of human beings) can be coercive or abusive, subtly and tacitly, even when they have no formal authority to be so.

Second, sports (and other) clubs, whose regulations are based on "consensual compact", are only rarely cause for concern, because their interests (and regulations) are limited and focused. Because religions encompass so much more, in one sense all of life, they can seem less like a group within society than an alternative to society. If this is so, their self-organisation can feel like an unacceptable threat to the rule of law.

Third, even when these two factors are not in play, a liberal society which treats individualised human rights as the centre of gravity around which other rights, such as group rights, orbit will often naturally doubt and undermine those group rights, and view with suspicion all groups (but especially religious ones) that claim those rights.

In this way, the potential for tension and even conflict is present and understandable. However, it is important to recognise that without group rights, *individual* rights become attenuated and vulnerable. Thus, if my right to live my life is limited to those activities that do not entail my forming self-organising groups (as opposed to loose affiliations), it is severely circumscribed. I become free to do what I want, as long as I do it alone. Moreover, our natural human tendency to form groups means that their restriction, in the name of equality or of liberty, results in an invasive and hyperactive state, involving itself in areas where it has, at best, only a limited role.

> *Were the organisational life of the community not protected by Article 9 of the Convention, all other aspects of the individual's freedom of religion would become vulnerable.*

Encouragingly, this is sometimes recognised in legal judgement. In *Hasan and Chaush v. Bulgaria*, in which the Bulgarian government intervened forcibly in the election of the Grand Mufti of the Bulgarian Muslims, the ECtHR noted that

> the autonomous existence of religious communities is indispensable for pluralism in a democratic society…it directly concerns not only the organisation of the community as such but also the effective enjoyment of the right to freedom of religion by all its active members. Were the organisational life of the community

not protected by Article 9 of the Convention, all other aspects of the individual's freedom of religion would become vulnerable.[15]

More noteworthy than this decision, albeit with no purchase in English law, was the decision reached by the US Supreme Court in *Hosanna-Tabor Evangelical Lutheran Church and School v. Equal Employment Opportunity Commission* in 2012.

> *"The autonomy of religious groups has often served as a shield against oppressive civil laws."*

The US has long recognised what is known as the 'ministerial exception', the right for religious organisations to appoint whom they choose without falling foul of anti-discrimination legislation. There were, however, certain outstanding questions[16] and loopholes[17] within the 'exception'. These came before the US Supreme Court in the *Hosanna* case. Here, most unusually, the Court reached a unanimous decision in favour of the church, reiterating not only that "the Establishment Clause…prohibits government involvement in such ecclesiastical decisions", but observing, in Justice Alito's concurring opinion, that "the autonomy of religious groups, both here in the United States and abroad, has often served as a shield against oppressive civil laws."[18]

This can irk modern sensibilities, particularly liberal universalist ones, in as far as it results in the protection of forms of self-organisation that they find objectionable. However, the core of a liberal society is one that resists the temptation to implement whatever conception of morality is fashionable at the moment through law, or to construct and secure a morally-harmonious society.[19] Rather, in the words of the ECtHR in a similar case, "the role of the authorities in such circumstances is not to remove the cause of tension by eliminating pluralism, but to ensure that the competing groups tolerate each other".[20]

The right for religious groups to self-organise is, thus, recognised in law, not simply for negative reasons – because a liberal society is under obligation to do so – but for positive ones – because a liberal society is itself protected and sustained by the liberty of such groups.

There is, however and inevitably, some disagreement about what this entails in practice. At one end, the decisions are straightforward. There is limited controversy concerning the rights of religious groups "to train, appoint, elect, or designate by succession, appropriate leaders called for by the requirements and standards of any religion or belief,"[21] or to establish seminaries and religious schools, and to prepare and distribute texts. This sort of self-government angers only the most doctrinaire secularists.

Similarly, there is widespread agreement on the general principle of non-interference, particularly in the US where the state's interest in eradicating discrimination has repeatedly been weighed against the interests of religious freedom and found wanting. Broadly speaking, the state is reluctant to become involved in disputes that are internal to religious communities, or to adjudicate between parties in religious disputes, on both principled and practical grounds. In the words of one American judge, "It is axiomatic that the guidance of the state cannot substitute for that of the Holy Spirit and that a courtroom is not the place to review a church's determination of 'God's appointed.'"[22] Accordingly, the principle of non-justiciability – refusing to settle such a dispute in the courts – goes back a long way in English law and is applied today to disputes within non-Christian religions, just as much as it was to disputes within Christian denominations.[23]

> "It is axiomatic that the guidance of the state cannot substitute for that of the Holy Spirit and that a courtroom is not the place to review a church's determination of 'God's appointed.'"

In reality, this is not unreservedly the case and in exceptional circumstances the courts will intervene, usually to enforce the laws of a religious group where there is a financial interest or a matter concerning the disposal of property. Nevertheless, even here the interference tends explicitly to follow the rules and regulations of the religious group in question and avoid arbitrating on the substance of those rules.[24]

At one end of the spectrum, therefore, there is much agreement concerning the freedom of religious groups to self-organise. The question is similarly largely uncomplicated at the other end of the spectrum. When the then chair of the Equality and Human Rights Commission, Trevor Phillips, commented in a Religion and Society Research Programme debate in 2012 that religious rules should stop "at the door of the temple", he was wrong on (at least) two accounts. Public law does not start at the temple door any more than religious law stops at it. A crime is not made legal simply because it is committed within a place of worship.

That much, then, is clear. But where the boundary between these two poles lies is far from straightforward, and becomes more complicated still when public (i.e. taxpayers') money is involved. In these circumstances, the chorus of voices saying that religious organisations must relinquish their self-organising principles when drawing on public money to provide public services, can become a clamour. In response, it is often pointed out that the religious people, who comprise religious groups, also pay tax, and to prevent them from participating in public life with integrity is itself discriminatory. Just as religious people should not be compelled to speak secular Esperanto when engaged in public life, nor should religious groups be compelled to relinquish all principles of self-organisation when engaged in public service.

This is an area where religious freedom does presently appear to be limited. The law does permit organised religions to discriminate on certain grounds that would not otherwise be allowed under the Equalities Act, but the terms are self-consciously narrow. Paragraph 790 within the Explanatory Notes to the Equality Act 2010 states that

> This specific exception applies to employment for the purposes of an organised religion, *which is intended to cover a very narrow range of employment*: ministers of religion and a small number of lay posts, including those that exist to promote and represent religion.[25]

More generally, organisations with a religious ethos can discriminate and "may wish to restrict applicants for the post of head of [their organisations] to those people that adhere to that faith," on the basis that "the person in charge of that organisation must have an in-depth understanding of the religion's doctrines."[26] However, the relevant note goes on to say, "other posts that do not require this kind of in-depth understanding, such as administrative posts, should be open to all people regardless of their religion or belief."

There is a certain logic to this, rooted in the desire to prevent discrimination, in the pejorative sense of that word. However, the result is that the balance is clearly tilted towards a weaker view of religious corporate freedom, in which the means of self-organising are circumscribed, and in some cases are prohibited unless permitted, rather than being permitted unless they are prohibited.

Stronger views are possible. In their book *Religious Freedom in the Liberal State*, Rex Ahdar and Ian Leigh advocate that "religious bodies have the right to reject candidates for ministry or discipline or expel an existing pastoral minister even if the grounds for doing so appear to liberals (and others) to be archaic, illiberal, or bigoted."[27] This, they acknowledge, is a "strong version" of religious group autonomy, and it is doubtful whether many people would advocate this level of freedom for religions participating in public life (i.e. for all posts in religious organisations, rather than ministers and pastors alone). That said, Trevor Phillips' view that religious 'law' (however that is understood) should stop at the temple door is unacceptable, compelling religious groups to adopt the secular veil when walking out in public.

If the principles outlined in the first part of this essay are right and, more specifically, if it is right that there is no automatic hierarchy in which group rights must always be subservient to individual rights, or vice versa, the presenting question in this section – should religious groups be free to run according to their own rules? – will not, and should not, get a straight answer. The issue is not whether the answer should be 'yes' or 'no', but whether it should be 'yes but…' or 'no except…' At the moment, the legal situation seems to be closer to the latter than the former, perhaps because concern for 'equality' has outweighed concern for 'liberty', or because a late-modern society such as ours thinks more naturally in terms of individuals (and individual rights) than it does groups (and group rights).

Whatever the reason, the danger is that a consistent answer of 'no except…' is liable not only to limit religious liberty in public life, licensing it just so long as it is sufficiently close to a liberal worldview not to disturb it, but also, in the long run, to hollow out the space between state and individual, as all substantive efforts at civil self-organisation are caught in a pincer movement between individuals' rights and the state that secures them.

The great leap forward in the English (latterly British) legal mind came with John Locke's enormously influential *Letter Concerning Toleration*, published in 1689. This argued convincingly, and from deep and explicit first (biblical) principles, that morality and legality were different things and to attempt to secure the former by means of the latter was a mistake. It would be a tragedy of the 21st century if an apparent concern for human liberty were to lead to the attempt to impose liberal morality through illiberal laws, thereby reversing the process initiated by Locke over 300 years ago.

> *[The] view that religious 'law' should stop at the temple door is unacceptable, compelling religious groups to adopt the secular veil when walking out in public.*

2.3 should religious groups be free to operate their own legal systems?

The question of whether religious groups should have their own legal systems is, in effect, a subset of the previous question and should properly be treated there. However, the sheer sensitivity of this question in Britain today, in the light of sharia law and Rowan Williams' famous 2008 lecture 'Civil and Religious Law in England – a Religious Perspective', means that it merits its own, short, section.[28]

Two initial points are worth bearing in mind. The first is that the question of religious legal systems is not exclusive to Islam. The Church of England has its own ecclesiastical law. The Roman Catholic Church has a Code of Canon Law, the justification for which John Paul II eloquently expounded in his Promulgation of the New Code of Canon Law in 1983.[29] Orthodox Jews have long had their own courts, known as Beth Din, in which they may settle certain civil disputes.

Nor, as a matter of fact, is it necessarily even an exclusively religious issue. Native American communities have been granted a supplementary jurisdiction in Canada, with a similar power of civil disputes. The question of 'supplementary' (N.B. not 'parallel') legal jurisdictions – or 'minority legal orders' as they are also known – is neither new nor narrow, and is certainly not – or rather should not be – a cipher for a debate about Islam itself.

The second point is that these legal 'systems' (the term itself is somewhat inexact) are not the same. The Church of England serves as a public authority, i.e. on behalf of the state, and its law is incorporated into English law. Church of England and Roman Catholic Canon Law is primarily focused on the regulation of ecclesiastical affairs – government, ministry, discipline, doctrine, liturgy, property, ecumenical relations, and the like – rather than civil ones. It is not, therefore, simply the case that accepting religious legal systems in principle means accepting religious legal systems, still less all religious legal systems, in practice.

The principles for accepting religious legal systems are the same as those of self-organisation outlined in the previous section. As Rowan Williams noted, people's social identities are not constituted by one exclusive set of relations or mode of belonging. Living a within a religious jurisdiction is in principle no different from operating within a set of club rules. As already noted, the rules and structures of religious associations are binding on assenting members through the doctrine of 'consensual compact' in the same way that they are with other membership groups. The Arbitration Act 1996 allows for disputes to be determined by religious courts and for their decisions to be recognised under State Law, on the basis of certain carefully articulated criteria. All parties involved need to demonstrate their genuine and willing assent to submit to such arbitration, in writing, with minors prohibited from participating, arbitrators complying with certain standards, and the whole process subject "to such safeguards as are necessary in the public interest."

The furore surrounding Rowan Williams' lecture was due, at least in part, to the fact that the public widely understood sharia law to be repressive, archaic and often brutal. Williams acknowledged such concerns and – ironically, given the response to the lecture – spent much of the talk outlining and offering responses to such legitimate objections. Thus, recognising a supplementary jurisdiction (whether religious or not) could not entail "a liberty to exert a sort of local monopoly in some areas"; in other words, there could be no legal divide "at the temple door", no legal ghettoization. Similarly, no supplementary jurisdiction could have the power "to deny access to the rights granted to other citizens or to punish its members for claiming those rights". Supplementary jurisdiction has to be supplementary and not parallel or alternative. Moreover they had to be voluntary and not coercive.

Perhaps most obviously in the context of sharia law, recognising supplementary jurisdictions could not mean colluding "with unexamined systems that have oppressive effect". Of course, what exactly constitutes "oppressive effect" is far from straightforward – hence the seemingly intractable debate about women who voluntary wear religiously-sanctioned clothing, such as the veil, but which others judge to be thoroughly oppressive. Such problems of judgement and definition notwithstanding, the caveat remains an essential one: no supplementary jurisdiction that was demonstrably dehumanising could be recognised, no matter how sincere or heartfelt its adherents were.

If such criteria can be met, there is no reason why society cannot come to a form of what Williams called transformative accommodation with such supplementary jurisdictions: "a scheme in which individuals retain the liberty to choose the jurisdiction under which they will seek to resolve certain carefully specified matters", such as "aspects of marital law, the regulation of financial transactions and authorised structures of mediation and conflict resolution."

Although areas such as sharia-compliant finance are often cited here, it is perhaps 'aspects of marital law' that are uppermost in this issue. Because family relations are so central to our identity and flourishing, this is naturally the area in which people feel a pressing need to be able to live according to their own religious commitments. This is not especially easy for British Christians to grasp, given that marriage and family law has been singularly formed by Christianity for centuries. However, it is possible that if the ethical foundations beneath family law do de-Christianise over coming years, Christians may seek to recognise a greater freedom for couples and families to enter into commitments and resolve disputes in a way that better reflects their own religious and ethical commitments. In this way, it is right that the desire among some religious minority communities to do this today is not simply dismissed out of hand but treated seriously, if qualifying criteria such as those outlined in Williams' lecture can be met.

That however is a big 'if' and it is quite possible to favour the principle of supplementary jurisdictions and yet come to the conclusion that they are practically unworkable in some circumstances or even practically unworkable altogether. In itself, this constitutes a good example of how one can treat different groups differently without being unfair or discriminatory (in the pejorative sense). If there is good evidence that some people or groups within a particular supplementary jurisdiction are being coerced, into judgements or into the jurisdiction itself; or that they are being denied the right of appeal or exit; or if there is no coercion at play but the minority legal order itself entails commitments or practices that are objectively dehumanising – then it is perfectly right and just to refuse to recognise that jurisdiction.

Ultimately, therefore, the response to the presenting question in this section becomes as much an empirical issue as a theoretical one. One's answer to the question of whether religious groups should be free to operate their own legal systems will necessarily depend on whether one finds those legal systems to be consonant with the safeguards necessary for their operation in a liberal democracy. And, as Professor Maleiha Malik pointed out in her essay on Minority Legal Orders in the companion volume to this essay,

> there are considerable empirical gaps in our understanding of the way in which the substantial norms are being adapted, interpreted and applied in minority legal orders. We know very little about the experience of users of MLOs.[30]

Whatever answer one does arrive at, however, it is worth highlighting a – perhaps the – crucial point of Williams' original lecture, which was lost in the ensuing media hysteria and which roots the partly-empirical question of this section, with the issues discussed in the last, and the principles outlined in part 1. "Citizenship in a secular society," the Archbishop remarked, "should not necessitate the abandoning of religious discipline, any more than religious discipline should deprive one of access to liberties secured by the law of the land." Put in the terms we have been using so far, this suggests that the communal identity and rights that derive from our spiritual nature are not negated by obedience to government, any more than the rights and responsibilities of citizenship are negated by religious identity.

> *The communal identity and rights that derive from our spiritual nature are not negated by obedience to government, any more than the rights and responsibilities of citizenship are negated by religious identity.*

2.4 should other beliefs be classed the same as religion? †

The principles outlined in the first part of this essay make it clear that any consideration of religious freedom that is grounded in Christian thought must include freedom to hold and, within limits, practice other (i.e. non-Christian) religious beliefs, and the freedom to hold, and practice, none. As part of their commitment to the gospel and the freedom it affords, Christians should be willing to fight for religious freedoms as a whole, rather than Christian freedoms alone.

This does not, it should be emphasised, mean ignoring the specificities of religious oppression. The persecution of Christians globally has rightly been called "an unfashionable crime against humanity" – because so little is it known or spoken about in educated Western circles – and it is entirely right and proper that certain Christian organisations should wish to focus specifically on the plight of their ill-treated brethren.[31] Nevertheless, the point remains that Christians should in principle be as willing to support the cause of non-believers who are persecuted for their beliefs, as they would hope secularists would

---

†   This section owes a great deal to Russell Sandberg's essay 'A Question of Belief' in Nick Spencer (ed.) *Religion and Law* (London: Theos, 2012)

be of, say, the freedoms championed by Christian Solidarity Worldwide. Religious freedom must, of necessity, also mean the freedom not to be religious.[32]

That much is clear. What is far less self-evident is how far freedom of religion should extend to systems of belief that have not historically been considered religious. This is an increasingly complex and pressing issue in Britain.

Article 9 of the European Convention on Human Rights provides for the "freedom to change…religion or belief and freedom…to manifest…religion or belief." The original EU Framework Directive offered no definition of "religion or belief", with the result that the phrase was initially interpreted as "any religion, religious belief, or similar philosophical belief".[33] Initially that "similar" was used to exclude beliefs – such as nationalist[34] or political[35] ones – that, despite being sincerely held, did not lie within a recognisable category of religion.

That changed in 2006, however, when, apparently to appease those who professed non-religious beliefs and objected to their beliefs being regarded as being religion-like, the word "similar" was removed and belief was now defined as "any religious or philosophical belief".[36] The word was judged superfluous in the context, with Baroness Scotland, then Minister of State for the Criminal Justice system and Law Reform, arguing that case law had suggested that certain criteria – such as cogency, seriousness, cohesion and importance – were sufficient to judge which "beliefs" were worthy of respect and which were not. Thus, she argued, by this reckoning secular humanism would pass the test but not the support of a political party or being of the Jedi 'religion'.[37]

Subsequent history has shown this to be optimistic, or naïve. In the words of legal scholar Russell Sandberg,

> the removal of the word 'similar'…deprived tribunal chairs of the (admittedly crude) methodology that they had developed for determining where the line was to be drawn – namely, by asking whether it was 'similar' to a religious belief or not – without providing any guidance as to what approach was to be taken instead.[38]

The result has been something of a mess as courts have struggled to draw lines in place of the (albeit blurred and faint) ones that had been erased with the deletion of the word 'similar'.

On the one hand, the justification for protecting a belief needed to be more than simply subjective. It wasn't enough for someone to feel very strongly about something. In the words of Lord Nicholls, to be protected in this way "a belief must satisfy some modest, objective minimum requirements".[39] Moreover, it needed to be coherent "in the sense of being intelligible and capable of being understood," rather than simply a miscellany of philosophical profundities.[40]

On the other hand, the same judge remarked that such "threshold requirements" should not be set too high. "Too much should not be demanded in this regard." Beliefs change, are often held as intuitively as they are reflectively, and are by no means always amenable to articulation and explanation. "Individuals cannot always be expected to express themselves with cogency or precision."[41] One should not demand of a believer epistemological sophistication to grant them credibility. Moreover, some judges have questioned whether the courts should (except in extreme cases) seek to "to impose an evaluative filter" at all, arguing that for "the Court to adjudicate on the seriousness, cogency and coherence of theological beliefs is…to take the Court beyond its legitimate role."[42]

Whether this is so or not, courts have been required to rule on the issue and, since 2009, many have taken their cue from an Employment Appeal Tribunal which found that belief in man-made climate change, together with the alleged resulting moral imperatives arising from it, was capable of constituting a "philosophical belief".[43] In this, Mr Justice Burton outlined five requirements as constituting a workable definition of "philosophical belief", namely that:

1. The belief must be genuinely held.

2. It must be a belief and not…an opinion or viewpoint based on the present state of information available.

3. It must be a belief as to a weighty and substantial aspect of human life and behaviour.

4. It must attain a certain level of cogency, seriousness, cohesion and importance.

5. It must be worthy of respect in a democratic society, be not incompatible with human dignity and not conflict with the fundamental rights of others.[44]

These five criteria have subsequently become the guidelines for evaluations in this area, employment tribunal chairs applying them as if they were a statutory test. They have not necessarily added to the clarity of the debate, however, partly because there still remains considerable (indeed greater) uncertainty over what does and does not constitute a belief worthy of protection, and partly because they have extended the category in a way that many instinctively feel is stretching the term 'belief' beyond what it should bear in the circumstance.

Thus, in 2007, in *Whaley v Lord Advocate*, Lord Hope of Craighead rejected the appellant's contention that hunting with hounds constituted a non-religious belief.[45] Four years later, in *Hashman v Milton Park (Dorset) Ltd*, it was found that a belief in the sanctity of life, comprising in particular of anti-foxhunting beliefs, *did* constitute a philosophical belief for the purpose of religious discrimination laws.[46] Hunting did not constitute a 'belief' worthy of protection, but anti-hunting did.

Two years earlier, in 2009, in *Greater Manchester Police Authority v Power*[47] the court had found that a belief in spiritualism and life after death and psychic powers was capable of being a 'belief'. In 2011, in *Maistry v The BBC* Justice Hughes found that a belief "that public service broadcasting has the higher purpose of promoting cultural interchange and social cohesion" constituted a "philosophical belief" because it met the *Grainger PLC v Nicholson* tests.[48]

The question of whether political beliefs merit such protection is a particularly vexed one. The judge in *Grainger PLC v Nicholson* remarked that the Attorney General suggested in parliament that "support of a political party" might not meet the description of a philosophical belief. "That must surely be so," Justice Burton said, "but that does not mean that a belief in a political philosophy or doctrine would not qualify. [A] belief in the political philosophies of Socialism, Marxism, Communism or free-market Capitalism might qualify."[49] Against that view, it was subsequently held, in *Unison v Kelly*[50], that the Marxist/Trotskyite beliefs held by trade union members of the Socialist Party did not constitute a "philosophical belief", although the judgment was such that the ambiguity over the status of political beliefs remained high, and "case law now suggests that some political beliefs may be protected."[51]

There is no clear or obvious 'solution' to this confusion and, for all that the principles outlined in the first half of this essay provide a cogent basis for protecting religious and non-religious beliefs and practices, within certain limits, they do not provide the clear definition of the category of religion which this matter needs. They do however point towards beliefs (and practices) that are grounded and focused *on ultimate concerns*.

It could be argued that the expansion of the belief category in recent jurisprudence merely reflects the fact that, in a less traditionally religious society such as ours, people's ultimate concerns are as, if not more, likely to be 'secular' than spiritual. Nevertheless, even if it were the case, the danger is that incorporating such beliefs into the category of 'religion and belief' threatens to broaden it to such an extent that it becomes unmanageable or meaningless.

Moreover, it seems unarguable that certain political beliefs pass the belief test, in terms of being genuine, cogent, serious, coherent, important, etc., and as such merit, and will receive, the protection of belief. Yet this in turn threatens to mute the criticism of such political views on which a liberal society is founded.

In short, the expansion of non-religious beliefs meriting protection to those substantial and coherent worldviews which are clearly 'similar' to religion – at least in terms of their ultimate or teleological concerns which are understood as alternatives to traditional religions – is not only acceptable but necessary as part of true religious freedom. However, the further expansion to encompass those beliefs which are genuine, cogent, serious and coherent, but do not engage with these 'similar' teleological concerns is liable to make the category of religious belief unwieldy and unworkable.

To refuse the label and protection of 'belief' to non-religious 'beliefs' of this nature, whether political or environmental for example, is not to denigrate or demean them, still less to insinuate that they were not worthy of respect and consideration. Rather, it is an acknowledgement of people's intrinsic *spiritual* nature (which, of course entails the possibility of rejecting that nature) and, importantly, to recognise that, however difficult it is to define precisely, this category of what we might call "religious or similar non-religious beliefs" is a legitimate category, and should not be dissolved into a wider, more amorphous category of belief in general.

As a coda to the (somewhat theoretical) question of whether other beliefs should be classed the same as religion, it is worth noting that, in *practical* terms, the question of whether religious and non-religious beliefs be understood and treated the same way is circumvented by recognising that the key question, at least when it comes to the workplace, is whether the belief in question is *relevant* to the job in question and, in particular, to the individual's competence to discharge their responsibilities.

This cuts through the theoretical Gordian knot. What matters is not so much how one categorises the belief under discussion as how that belief is relevant to the situation in question. It may be the case that religious beliefs are more likely to be relevant than non-religious ones, tending, as they do, to be more comprehensive. Whether or not that is so, however, this practical response treats the demarcation of religious from non-religious beliefs as less relevant than the way in which either interacts with the job. Such an approach therefore admits social pluralism in the workplace without denying the employer the right to organise and recruit according to its own relevant criteria.[52]

2.5 should religious people be protected from, or prevented from giving, offence?

At first glance, this question, of all those posed in the second half of this essay, seems to merit the shortest and simplest response: no.

The idea that giving or taking offence at a religious matter should be a legal issue seems to be little more than a throwback to earlier, more brutal times, when the church was (all but) synonymous with the state, and therefore to blaspheme was, in effect, to speak a form of treason.

That tight symbiosis began to loosen over 300 hundred years ago in Britain and by the mid-1880s it became clear that publication of anti-Christian work was not prosecutable. Blasphemy legislation was thereafter little in evidence, and although Mary Whitehouse successfully used it against *Gay News* in 1979, the fact that both the then Archbishop of Canterbury, Donald Coggan, and Cardinal Basil Hume declined the invitation to give evidence at this trial strongly suggested the direction of travel.

The publication of Salman Rushdie's *The Satanic Verses*, and the ensuing violent protests about its blasphemous nature did not materially change anything – attempts at a private prosecution were refused on grounds that blasphemy laws only applied to Christianity – but it did complicate matters, introducing the spectre of race hatred and violence into an area that had heretofore been more straightforwardly 'religious'.

A further unsuccessful private prosecution, this time for Channel 4's screening of *Jerry Springer: The Opera* in 2005, suggested that blasphemy was a dormant rather than a dead law, and so the law was finally abolished, in a single sentence with little protest, as part of the Criminal Justice and Immigration Act 2008.

Legally, therefore, the story seems to have come to an end – at least in Britain. (It is worth noting that blasphemy legislation still exists in a number of European countries, including Austria, Denmark, Finland, Greece, Italy and the Netherlands, that it was introduced to the Republic of Ireland in 2009, and that the European Court of Human Rights has regularly upheld laws criminalising blasphemy on grounds of them being necessary for the protection of others). But it is worth exploring why Christians should be content with this arrangement, first as a means of showing that there are authentically Christian reasons to reject blasphemy legislation, and second because it may help navigate the still-choppy – and, post-*Satanic Verses*, more uncertain – waters of religious offence.

The first point to make is that no Christian will think blasphemy is a good thing, for reasons that do not need articulating. A follower of Christ will not only seek to avoid degrading the sacred but may well endeavour to persuade others likewise. That protected sacred should extend beyond Christian commitments. Disagreeing with other religious convictions, even profoundly, is not reason for mocking and denigrating them. At the very least, therefore, if Christians were to favour the legal protection of the Christian sacred, they should do the same for other concepts of the holy.

However, the idea that such protection should be afforded by the state, i.e. by coercion, is misguided. At the heart of the Christian story is an act of self-emptying and vulnerability, and towards the culmination of that story, in Gethsemane, is an encounter in which Christ explicitly refuses to let violence stand in his defence. The result is not the protection, but the humiliation and degradation, of the Word made flesh.

> *There is something distasteful about those who enthusiastically fight for the right to mock, humiliate, and degrade that which others judge precious. In this sense, blasphemy is a toxic right.*

The point is reinforced by Paul in 1 Corinthians, when he rhetorically asks his audience, "What business is it of mine to judge those outside the church?" His mind is on people behaving, rather than speaking, immorally, but the point stands: passing judgement, especially through law, on those outside the church, for failing to meet Christian standards of respect for the sacred is wrong (not to mention impractical and counter-productive). Thus, when Mary Whitehouse said that she took *Gay News* to court because "I simply had to protect Our Lord", she demonstrated a severe confusion firstly over what was needed to protect whom, and secondly what responsibility she had to judge those outside the church.[53]

This is the model by means of which Christians can spurn the law of blasphemy: love of God does not need, indeed cannot need, coercion as a bulwark; fidelity to the Word cannot be grounded on exercise of the sword. At the risk of repetition, this does not mean that blasphemy is acceptable, still less admirable. There is indeed something distasteful about those who enthusiastically fight for the right to mock, humiliate, and degrade that which others judge precious. In this sense, blasphemy is a toxic right.

This distinction may help understand the more complicated landscape of offence that emerged from the shadow of *The Satanic Verses* and the presence of a different kind of religious sensibility within British culture.

The original blasphemy laws were grounded, in part, in the understanding that attacking God was also attacking the nation that was constituted under him: blasphemy, as noted, was a form of treason. That association was unwound over the 19th century in particular and by the 20th it was recognised that giving religious offence did not entail political or social sedition. To attack God was not to attack the nation governed in his name, nor even to attack those who loved and worshipped him.

This dissociation became more problematic, however, in an age of unprecedented immigration and ethnic plurality, and as Islam became a prominent feature within the social landscape. To offend, deliberately and provocatively, a religion might – conceivably – be to attack religious people.

Thus, at about the same time that it abolished blasphemy, the government was introducing offences outlawing religious hatred and religiously aggravated offences. These were motivated by the terrorist attacks of 2001 and 2005, the wars in Afghanistan and Iraq, and the ensuing febrile atmosphere, in which there was widespread anger, and the very real threat of violence conducted against and on behalf of Islam and Muslims.

In the event, the Racial and Religious Hatred Act 2006 took four attempts and five years to get on statute book, being severely circumscribed in the process, with religious and secular groups coming together to combat the government's original intention to include "abusive and insulting" words or behaviour as an offence. The potential here to blur the distinction between attacking a religion and attacking its adherents was significant and, eventually, the commitment to protecting the former was signalled strongly in Section 29J of the Act which stated baldly that

> Nothing in this Part shall be read or given effect in a way which prohibits or restricts discussion, criticism or expressions of antipathy, dislike, ridicule, insult or abuse of particular religions or the beliefs or practices of their adherents, or of any other belief system or the beliefs or practices of its adherents, or proselytising or urging adherents of a different religion or belief system to cease practising their religion or belief system.[54]

Ultimately, the potential for the Racial and Religious Hatred Act to repeal the 'toxic right' of blasphemy was averted (although the result was that it was not immediately clear what the Act would cover that was not already covered by existing criminal offences) but the incident illustrates how the border between sin and crime might be easily erased. The logic famously and influentially articulated in John Locke's *Letter Concerning Toleration*, in which sin and crime were disambiguated and treated differently, is readily ignored when the powers that be claim a higher vision of the good – be it the preservation of Christian public order or, latterly, liberal, plural public order.

A similar example can be seen in the notorious example of Harry Hammond, an octogenarian, autistic, evangelical street evangelist who was convicted and fined £300 for speaking against homosexuality in public in 2001. His words offended many bystanders and a hostile crowd gathered round him, some of whom threw soil at and poured water on him. Someone tried to seize his placard sign and Hammond was knocked to the ground, and yet it was he who was arrested and charged under section 5 of Public Order Act 1986 and convicted. Many people at the time, including the gay rights campaigner Peter

Tatchell, pointed out that such a use of the law was contrary to the stated right to give offence, Tatchell being willing to testify on Hammond's behalf.

Hammond's case may have been extreme but it was not wholly unique. Over the last ten years complaining to a council about its expenditure on gay rights, saying on radio that homosexual couples should not be permitted to adopt children, and publicly advocating that homosexual people should seek counselling have all been subject to police investigations on the basis of 'hate crime'.[55]

Neither the Racial and Religious Hatred Act nor the arrest of Harry Hammond was entirely egregious or without logic: the right to offend, whether religious or homosexual people, does need to be circumscribed by concerns for public order. However, once again, it is easy to see how this concern for public order can be used to limit that freedom to an illegitimate degree. Attempts to outlaw hatred, offence, abuse, and insulting words – however well-meaning they may be – now risk treating sinful activity as if it were criminal – ironically reversing the process Locke initiated.

The question of giving religious offence in Britain, seemingly so closed by the mid-20th century will now, it appears, run and run in the 21st, although with the focus shifted entirely from Christianity to Islam. The danger is the debate is caught painfully between those who will countenance not only no offence but no criticism of their religious beliefs, and those who, in response, take effort and pleasure at provoking them. This is not a recipe for social harmony.

The eventual Christian relinquishing of blasphemy legislation is wholly consistent with the gospel message of a saviour who eschewed violence when he was perfectly capable of preventing or at least limiting the harm done to him. Much as Christians may despair at the sophomoric attempts to blaspheme them into a reaction, they should not respond. But if they should not be legally protected from offence (or indeed from giving it, not that they should wish to), they still need to be alert to the way in which attacking and ridiculing a person's idea of the sacred can, in extreme cases, shade over into attacking them.

2.6 how far should the religious be free to manifest their religion?

The question of how far religious people should be able to manifest their religious commitments – alongside the parallel question, dealt with below, of how far they should have exemption from equality legislation – has become the focus of contemporary debates around religion and law. For all the fuss there was over Rowan Williams' sharia lecture, it was a short, sudden storm when compared with the various small showers regarding the right to manifest one's religious faith, many of which have lasted long and drifted, eventually, across the channel to the European Court of Human Rights.[56]

The most iconic of these was *Eweida v British Airways plc* in which a British Airways employee was prohibited from wearing a cross necklace at work. Eweida eventually won her case but in the 6½ years between her first being asked to cover up the offending jewellery and the European Court delivering its verdict, the case came, for many, to epitomise the anti-religious – or more precisely anti-Christian – bias of the law, or, conversely, among some imaginative secularists, the perils of Christian zealotry.[57]

The danger with iconic cases is that detail and nuance are often left behind as the subject is painted in bold primary colours. The issue becomes one of oppression vs. bigotry, or wrong vs. right. This is particularly perilous in the question of manifestation as the devil is in the detail, so to speak, and the response to the presenting question will, and should, differ, according to the kind of manifestation, its significance, its sincerity and its location – where in the social landscape is it happening.

significance and sincerity

As emphasised in the first part of this essay, whilst the freedom to hold and manifest religious beliefs should be taken seriously – and perhaps more seriously than a purely secular analysis is naturally inclined to do – it does not serve as a get-out-of-jail free card, trumping all other 'rights'. Much depends, it would appear, on what precisely is being manifested and how important that manifestation is to the underlying belief.

Intuitively this seems right: there are greater grounds for recognising core religious freedoms than peripheral ones. There is, for example, prima facie, a better case for recognising the freedom of acts that are scripturally commanded, than for those that are theologically recommended. "The weight to be given to religious rights may depend upon how close the subject-matter is to the core of the religion's values or organisation."[58] In one regard, this kind of judgement is unavoidable. As one judge in a case in Oregon remarked,

> dispensing with a 'centrality' inquiry is utterly unworkable. It would require, for example, the same degree of 'compelling state interest' to impede the practice of throwing rice at church weddings as to impede the practice of getting married in church.[59]

However, there is a difference in judging whether the appeal to religious scruple is opportunistic, disingenuous or vexatious, and judging whether it is sufficiently close to the alleged core of religious belief to merit legal respect. The former requires a relatively perfunctory assessment and is a low hurdle over which the manifestation has to pass. The latter approach, by comparison, invariably involves the courts in adjudicating what are core and what are peripheral manifestations and, as already noted, there are convincing principled and pragmatic reasons why the courts should not be involved with this.[60]

It is not so much the fact that such complex adjudication cannot be done well. When, for example, the question of open air cremations came before the courts in 2007-09, they received and relied on sensitive, intelligent and balanced evidence pertaining to the range and weight of different Hindu views concerning cremation.[61] It is rather that they can be, and sometimes are, done badly. Thus, in one of the cases that accompanied *Eweida* to the European Court in 2012/13, in which registrar Lillian Ladele refused to conduct civil partnerships for reasons of religious conscience, the Court of Appeal had ruled that "Ms Ladele's objection was based on her view of marriage, which was not a core part of her religion", and that therefore, "Islington's requirement in no way prevented her from worshipping as she wished."[62] Similarly, in the case of *Celestina Mba v Merton LBC*, the Employment Tribunal concluded that the appellant's "belief that Sunday should be a day of rest and worship upon which no paid employment was undertaken…is not a core component of the Christian faith."[63] The idea that the view of marriage or Sunday rest is peripheral to the Christian faith is, to put it generously, dubious.

Until quite recently, the European Court drew a distinction between 'manifestation' and 'motivation', to the effect that those actions that *manifested* a religious belief were deemed (more) worthy of protection than those that were merely motivated by religious belief. This distinction was not very different to the core vs. peripheral distinction, however, not only potentially entangling the courts in theological discussions but drawing implicitly on the conception that those actions that were *merely* motivated by religious faith were inherently private, or at least did not merit public protection, whereas others were not. Subsequent to this, there has been a shift towards assessing whether a manifestation is 'intimately linked' to a belief, although it is not clear whether this formulation would avoid the pitfalls already noted.

Similarly, in Celestina Mba's appeal against the original Employment Tribunal decision, the Appeal Judge recognised that there were "legal errors" in the reasoning of the Employment Tribunal, that more attention should have been paid to "the diversity of beliefs…within religions", and that it was undeniable that "for some Christians, working on Sundays is unacceptable". In doing so, he helped shift the focus away from the test of whether the practice in question is core to the religion as a whole (with all the difficulties of assessment that involves) to whether it was core for the believer in question; from whether it was 'objectively core', so to speak, to whether it was 'subjectively core'. That noted, the Employment Appeal Tribunal did not overturn the original decision in Ms Mba's case.[64]

location: private and public

In essence, then, while it is undoubtedly necessary to make some judgement on the nature of the religious manifestation, it would be better if all the judicial eggs were not put in this particular basket. Attention should be paid also to the social location of the manifestation as well the extent to which it is intimately linked to the belief in question. Whether the manifestation is within an institutional religious setting (such as a church or mosque); a religiously-affiliated setting (such as a religious charity); an institutional non-religious setting (such as a workplace); or the general public arena will affect the level of recognition and protection it merits in law.

We have already argued for a relatively high barrier for interference with the rules and principles of organised religious groups. Respect for both innate human spirituality and our natural group-forming tendencies means that although the state is perfectly within its right to interfere with religious organisations, it should do so sparingly and only with very good reason. In these instances, religious people should be able to manifest their beliefs quite comprehensively, wearing, saying, appointing and, to a large degree, doing as they see fit.

The public arena should not be seen as the polar opposite to that of religious institutions in this matter, i.e. if religious institutions are the forums in which believers may most fully manifest their religious beliefs, it is not the case that the public is the forum in which they can least do so. To think that would be to fall into the error of hard secularism. Religion it is not simply a private affair, happily confined to the home and places of formal worship.

The public is, however, a forum in which negotiation between different commitments and faiths is required, making limitations on religious manifestations necessary. Some of these are reasonably straightforward. The fêted case of Shambo the Bull, the temple bullock at the Hindu Monastery and Temple at Skanda Vale in Carmarthenshire, which contracted the bacterium that causes bovine tuberculosis, is a good example of this. The Skanda Vale Temple rejected the call to have Shambo killed and sought a reprieve. The monks' attitude to Shambo and, more generally, to the sanctity of life was undoubtedly earnest, coherent, cogent, and sufficiently central to their beliefs to merit protection. However, the plain public health hazard posed by the disease outweighed these factors and Shambo was put down.[65]

The case of open air funeral pyres, already referred to, is an example of a more complex reasoning that the manifestation in public demands.[66] In this instance, there was no direct threat to public health. Moreover, it was recognised that, whatever the range of views on the subject within Hindu thought and culture, in this particular instance, the claimant's "personal perception" of the matter amounted to "an obligation, derived from scriptural texts, to be burned on an open air funeral pyre after his death"; in other words a legitimate manifestation of the claimant's religious beliefs. The fact that that "typically Hindus in this country do not share that belief", was "beside the point". The case for such pyres was therefore stronger than for Shambo.

However, the judge also felt he had to take into consideration the views of the Secretary of State for Justice, who was an interested party in the case, to the effect that "others in the community would be upset and offended…and would find it abhorrent that human remains were being burned in this way."[67] The right not to be offended is not much of a right, of course, but in this instance this was not just a matter of personal umbrage being taken but the conviction, among elected officials, that public taste would be sufficiently offended to merit legislation (admittedly now a century old) against open air funeral pyres. The conviction of elected officials is hardly an infallible guide itself: after all, it is not unknown for elected officials to respond to public opinion for reasons other than disinterested justice. However, on this occasion it was deemed sufficiently secure for the court to feel it "must accord primacy to the conclusion of elected representatives…[and] conclude that a significant number of people would find cremation on open air pyres a matter of offence."

Were it not for this, the judge argued, the claimant's freedom to manifest his religious belief in open air funeral pyres was permissible. Moreover, the judgement raised the possibility that "with time, education and publicity the public will not be offended but will recognise that open air funeral pyres are a practice worthy of respect." In other words, decisions of this nature, which take into account public feeling, are mutable. However, in the current social climate, the conclusion was that open air pyres, while being an example of a cogent and important manifestation of religious belief in public, could be banned for reasons of public opinion.

Shambo and open-air cremation are good examples not only of the increasing range of religious manifestation cases that come before the courts but of judgements where the default position is for the freedom to manifest religious beliefs in public, which is denied only for good reasons, such as public health or order.

It is worth noting here, in parenthesis, that this is not simply a religious issue, and that cases concerning the manifestation of non-religious views in public are far from unheard of. For example, over thirty years ago, one Miss Arrowsmith claimed that her distribution leaflets to soldiers, urging them to decline service in Northern Ireland, was simply the legitimate manifestation of her pacifist views.[68] The European Court, however, found that neither the actual contents of the leaflets, nor the fact of their distribution, constituted a straightforward manifestation of Arrowsmith's pacifism but were rather a political statement that could be seen as an encouragement or incitement to disaffection among soldiers. The question of legitimate manifestation of belief in public is not simply a religious one.

location: institutional

The question shifts once more when the location is moved away from religious institutions or the public arena, to bodies within civil society, such as schools or workplaces. This is where it is particularly important for religious thought in this matter to maintain consistency, as there is a temptation to have one's cake and eat it. What I mean by this is that one cannot, with integrity, argue for the right of religious institutions to run according to their own logic, and then deny the right of other groups within civil society to do so. More specifically, one cannot simply use the religious manifestation card against the rules and regulations of different groups, whether in the public or private sector, in which religious people find themselves.

This is emphatically not the same as saying that Christians (or Muslims, etc.) must abandon their religious manifestations when they enter the workplace (or school, etc.) any more than they must do so when they enter the open public arena. Once again, faith cannot so readily be privatised. What it is to say is that here, perhaps above anywhere else, a particular degree of negotiation, reasonableness and accommodation is required.

The number of cases dealing with issues like these has multiplied over recent years. Some make the headlines. Many others do not. Lydia Playfoot was forbidden by her school from wearing a chastity ring which she argued was key to her Christian faith.[69] The court upheld the school's decision. Sarika Angel Watkins-Singh was prevented from her school from wearing a Sikh Kara bracelet.[70] The court overturned the school's decision. Shirley Chaplin, a nurse, was prevented from wearing a cross on a chain by the Royal Devon and Exeter NHS Trust. The Trust's decision, ultimately upheld by the European Court in the same judgement that overturned BA's ban on Nadia Eweida's wearing a cross on her uniform, found against Chaplin.[71] Shabina Begum was prevented by the school she attended from wearing "a long coat-like garment known as a jilbab", as it contravened the uniform policy. Ultimately – different courts having come to different conclusions – the House of Lords found for the school.[72] Aishah Azmi was prevented by the school at which she worked from wearing a niqab, which covered her face.[73] The Employment Appeal Tribunal found for the school. A Sikh prison officer was forbidden by SERCO and the Prison Service from wearing his kirpan, or ritual dagger, while on duty for reasons of prison security. The court found in favour of SERCO and the Prison Service. Mr Copsey, a team leader employed by Devon Clays, refused to work on a new seven-day employment pattern and although he indicated his willingness occasionally to work on a Sunday in a different role "if there was a genuine unexpected and unavoidable emergency", he was dismissed and lost his case.[74]

This is simply a tiny fraction of the number of recent religious cases where, in effect, the qualified right to manifest a religious belief has come up against the qualified right for an institution like a school, hospital, prison or workplace to organise itself.

> *There is no legal algorithm to solve such issues and a simple hierarchy of rights is an inadequately blunt device for sorting them.*

It will be clear from the above decisions that no one party always wins out. This is as it should be. Neither 'my' right to manifest my belief nor 'our' right to organise is automatically superior to the other. Nor, indeed, is my right to manifest my belief or our right to organise obviously the default position, from which judgements may occasionally defer. The balance may lie more naturally with one party in one instance and another in another depending on the facts of the case. There is no legal algorithm to solve such issues and a simple hierarchy of rights is an inadequately blunt device for sorting them.

That does not mean that decisions are necessarily arbitrary, and there are various guidelines that can help navigate the way we think about this precise issue. In some instances, the fact of public health or safety will decide the issue. While this is unlikely to be as clear as it was in, say, the case of Shambo the bull, Shirley Chaplin's case, in which the presence of a necklace, even with a quick release mechanism was judged a health risk in a hospital, is an example of how this consideration can take effect. (The fact that the Trust prohibited all front-line staff from wearing any type of necklace further strengthens their position in this case). The case of the prison officer banned from carrying a kirpan falls into a similar category as the presence of a dagger on a prison officer presents an obvious risk in that particular environment.

In other cases, even if there is no obvious public safety issue at play, it will be clear that institutional rules that are the point of tension are central to the existence of the institution itself and therefore hard to negotiate. This was the case for Aishah Azmi, whose wearing of a niqab may well have qualified as a coherent, sincere and important manifestation of her faith, but practically impeded her ability to discharge her educational duties. In this instance, the school's dress policy was not arbitrary or discriminatory but reasoned and necessary.

The same could not be said for the British Airways case. Although corporations place an emphasis on brand image for a good reason, with their staff playing a key role in that, it is doubtful whether corporate image should carry the same weight as school or hospital dress codes. Corporate images are, after all, highly malleable. Moreover, there is good evidence to believe that the maintenance of brand identity, although important, could not be of overriding significance to BA because it permitted exceptions for other religious clothing and, in any case, had abandoned the policy in the face of significant public criticism by the time of the hearing.[75]

Furthermore, there was no indication that Nadia Eweida could not discharge her duties when wearing her lapel cross, in the way that Aishah Azmi could not when wearing her niqab. In this regard, corporate dress policy is ultimately arbitrary and readily capable of accommodating the kind of religious manifestation required in this case.

The Eweida case turned, in some of the lower courts, on the question of whether a wearing a cross was a necessary manifestation of a person's religious faith. However, this question, as noted earlier, is fraught with difficulties. Even if it is addressed and answered coherently, it invariably tilts the ground towards more legalistic religious beliefs and away from those in which a public manifestation of belief may be desirable but is not mandatory. This, in effect, prioritises many non-Christian religious commitments over Christian ones, and particularly over Protestant ones, and this can easily, and not without reason, be seen as an example of legal imbalance.

This can be seen in the cases of Playfoot and Watkins-Singh. Playfoot lost her case in part because as the judge wrote, "the Claimant was under no obligation, by reason of her belief, to wear the ring; nor does she suggest that she was so obliged." Because "the act of wearing a ring is not 'intimately linked' to the belief in chastity before marriage", it was not deemed worthy of protection. By contrast, because the Kara bracelet is one of "the 5 Ks…the outward signs required of a Sikh…regarded as demonstrating both loyalty to the Gurus' teaching and the bravery to be counted at times when even their lives are endangered by this visibility," it was deemed worthy of protection. And yet, such a significance test aside, neither piece of jewellery (chastity ring or kara bracelet) is especially evident on the wearer (unlike, say, a niqab or jilbab), neither constituted a health risk, neither offended public opinion, and both clearly symbolised something of real importance to the wearer.

The result is a perceived imbalance in justice, predicated simply on the court's judgement of what is and isn't important or intimately linked to religious belief. In the light of this, it would be better for the court to limit its concern to ensuring that "an assertion of religious belief is made in good faith: 'neither fictitious, nor capricious, and that it is not an artifice,'" rather than to attempt to determine the significance of the manifestation to the believer in question.

> It is not for the court to embark on an inquiry into the asserted belief and judge its 'validity' by some objective standard such as the source material upon which the claimant founds his belief or the orthodox teaching of the religion in question or the extent to which the claimant's belief conforms to or differs from the views of

others professing the same religion. Freedom of religion protects the subjective belief of an individual.[76]

If we should respect the rights of institutions to self-organise, the schools in question clearly did have the right to design and implement their uniform policy. A good uniform policy in a school is as, arguably more, important than a good corporate uniform policy. However, this right should be tempered with sensitivity to the ethnic, cultural and religious commitments of both staff and pupils. It is, after all, a right that is intended ultimately to serve their good rather than, say, a corporate uniform policy in which the good of the wearer is a relatively small consideration.

Accordingly, one would hope for a degree of flexibility and accommodation in such policy. This is precisely what Denbigh High School had instituted before the case with Shabina Begum. The school offered three uniform options, one of which was a shalwar kameeze which had been worn by some Muslim, Hindu and Sikh female pupils at the school.[77] In addition to this, the school had, in 1993, appointed a working party to re-examine its dress code, which consulted parents, students, staff, and the Imams of the three local mosques, during which "there was no objection to the shalwar kameeze, and no suggestion that it failed to satisfy Islamic requirements." Irrespective of a school's right to set its uniform policy, the fact it had done so with this degree of flexibility and willing accommodation made its position all the stronger.[78]

It may be, in the cases of Lydia Playfoot and Watkins-Singh, that their respective schools has good reason to limit the wearing of jewellery and it could perhaps be argued that permitting jewellery on account of its religious significance might have made denying it for purely cosmetic reasons more difficult. However, it has been the contention of this essay that religious commitments are different to, and cannot simply be reduced to secular ones, and that therefore it is regrettable that, although the schools (thought they) had the right to set their uniform policies as they wished (in retrospect the courts ruled that only one of them did), it is regrettable they were unwilling to be more accommodating to these manifestations of religious belief.

timing

One final consideration is that of timing, i.e. whether the tension around a manifestation of religious belief arises on account of a change in views and behaviour of the religious person, or whether it arises on account of a change in employment or other conditions.

In the case of Mr Copsey, the Devon Clays employee, the difficulties arose as a result of increased business orders and production needs. Although businesses must be able to respond to market demands in this way, due attention should be paid to the fact that terms and conditions are changing around the employee, rather than vice versa. In contrast to this, Shabina Begum had worn the shalwar kameeze "happily and without complaint" for two years before the argument with Denbigh High School. Similarly, Aishah Azmi, according to the judgement, had worn a black tunic and headscarf with no face covering at interview and did not then indicate that her religious beliefs required her to wear a veil or placed any limitation on her working. The same consideration should have come into play in the case of Lillian Ladele, another of the cases that appeared with Eweida before the European Court in 2012/13.

None of this is to suggest that people cannot change their minds, or risk losing all their rights if they do, any more than that companies and institutions cannot change their terms of employment or uniform policies where there might be a conflict with religious employees. Rather, it simply underlines that due weight should be given to the existing agreement or situation that is being changed.

summary: 'reasonable accommodation' as a way forward

Overall, these guidelines do not solve the vexed questions that arise when claims for religious freedom, and in particular freedom to manifest religious belief, come into tension with institutional rules and guidelines. But that is primarily because this is not a soluble issue but rather a permanent feature of a plural liberal democracy. Taking into consideration the particular context of each case – the contract entered into, the legitimacy of a policy's aims, the degree of accommodation made available, etc – gestures in the direction of a 'proportionality' approach in which "the extent and seriousness of the infringement of the right [is] weighed against the importance of the conflicting interest and prohibits measures that impose a disproportionate impact." By addressing fact-specific contextual questions, such an approach tries to avoid "[making] one side a winner and another a loser permanently…[and tries to] resolve matters but without artificially ending debate on issues on which there is no agreement."[79]

This suggests that 'reasonable accommodation' is the most promising way forward in such difficult matters. Reasonable accommodation recognises the validity and importance of religious, and comparable non-religious, commitments and requires employers and other public bodies to accommodate them in as far as it is reasonable for them to do so. The idea will be familiar within English law from the duty of employers to make reasonable accommodation for employees with disabilities.[80] However, it has no status with regard to religion or belief, unlike Canada where it plays a significant role.

There, the bar is set high and employers are required to demonstrate "that they have made every effort to accommodate an employee and that it would be impossible to modify or eliminate a particular requirement without incurring undue hardship".[81] This requires a proportionality approach, setting up a balance "between the employee's arguments for accommodation and the employer's legitimate reasons in resisting accommodation."[82] There are (and have been) good arguments on both sides of this debate, and it has proven quite possible to turn down an employee's request for reasonable accommodation on religious grounds on the basis that to grant such accommodation was to make an undue and unsustainable demand on an employer or institution. However, reasonable accommodation does at least treat that request seriously enough to require a serious response from employers and public bodies.

Reasonable accommodation does not demand the abrogation of regulations or statutes but rather flexibility in the effort to minimise any discriminatory effects. It attempts to sidestep any hierarchy of rights and to avoid crowning social winners and losers through legal processes. Although it has been criticised as "the triumph of pragmatism over principle", this is hardly right as it does not bypass principles but merely softens their impact where possible, seeking "the maximum equitable co-existence between employer and employee."[83]

Interestingly and encouragingly, the Equality and Human Rights Commission has outlined its willingness, in response to consultation feedback, to explore the idea of reasonable accommodation as a "useful practical application in cases concerning the manifestation of religion or belief."[84] The Council of Europe's Commissioner for Human Rights has also commented that

> As part of the further development of this new generation of [national equality] legislation consideration needs to be given to extending the provisions on reasonable accommodation to the other grounds covered by the legislation and to reviewing the definition of discrimination. Reasonable accommodation could be further developed under the grounds of gender or sex, age, religion or belief, racial or ethnic origin, sexual orientation, gender identity and socio-economic status.[85]

It may be, then, that reasonable accommodation will play a greater role in dealing with these most contentious and intractable questions of freedom and equality. Such an approach would fit well with the guidelines laid out earlier – making only the minimum necessary judgement on the significance or theological justification of religious manifestations but paying close attention to the location of that manifestation; affording maximal freedom for religious manifestation within religious institutional settings; and adopting a default position of religious liberty in a public setting which can be limited but only with good reason. Between them, these offer a way of navigating the question of manifesting religious belief in way that is both principled and pays attention to the reality and sensitivities of different situations.

2.7 how should we reconcile religious freedom with equality legislation?

In much the same way as the question of religious legal systems is really a subset of the wider question of the extent to which religious groups should be able to operate according to their rules, the question of whether religious people should be free from the obligations of Equality Legislation is, in effect, a subset of the previous question regarding how far religious people should be free to manifest their beliefs. However, the sometimes ill-informed sensitivity surrounding 'equality', rather like the sometimes ill-informed sensitivity surrounding sharia, suggests that the question is worth a separate exploration.

The first point to make is that the way in which the presenting question is framed – deliberately in this case, because that is precisely how it is typically framed in popular discourse – is inherently prejudicial. Why should 'religious people' (who are…?) be free from obligations that are placed on 'the rest of us', especially when it comes to something as obviously right as 'equality'? Phrased this way, subtleties (such as the fact that the Equality Act designates "religion or belief" a "protected characteristic") are lost and the answer becomes obvious.

By this stage in this essay, it should be clear that equality does not mean treating everything as if it were the same, and that because religious faith is not something that can be reduced to and redescribed in secular terms, it may be perfectly just to offer exceptions to equality legislation under the right conditions. Thus, the debate invited by the presenting question may be better framed in the terms of the previous question, namely whether religious people should be free to manifest their beliefs.

In the light of that, some of the answers have already been discussed and are (relatively) uncontroversial. Religious groups are free to select their leaders, ministers and pastors, irrespective of equality legislation, for reasons outlined above (although it is worth repeating that those reasons are more widely accepted in the US, with its strong traditions of religious freedom, than they are in Britain).

The question becomes more vexed, however, when we move away from religious institutions and think about the provision of goods and services, particularly public services. Here the case of Lillian Ladele, removed by Islington Borough Council for refusing to conduct same-sex civil partnerships, has become iconic in the way that Eweida did regarding dress code, eventually accompanying it to the European Court of Human Rights in 2012-13. The Court found against Ladele, although uniquely among the four cases, it had two dissenting opinions, and it was widely considered to be the most finely balanced of the cases.

The Ladele case was readily painted in primary moral colours: homophobic bigotry vs. equality and justice. This is unfair, failing to recognise the nuances of this particular case. Ladele had been working for the council ruled since 1992, and had been a registrar of Births, Marriages and Deaths for more than three years before the Civil Partnership Act came into force. Ladele registered her concerns with her line-manager before the Act came into force. She was not alone in raising her fears (two other registrars did the same at Islington). When the 2004 Act finally came into force, Islington unilaterally designated all their registrars as civil partnership registrars. However, Ms Ladele managed to make informal arrangements with colleagues to swap assignments, so as to avoid the issue. The case only became a problem when, in March 2006, two gay registrars complained to the council that they felt "victimised" by Ms Ladele's decision, after which point the Council ruled that Ladele was in breach of its 'Dignity for All' equality and diversity policy. (It is worth noting that "no service user or prospective service user of the Borough seems to have ever complained." Ms Ladele also registered feeling victimised and picked on for her views within the council.[86]) Eventually, after Ms Ladele's two colleagues had pursued their complaint against her, her contract of employment was terminated.

> *This will be morally distasteful to some but that is precisely the sense that we should be experiencing in a liberal, plural society.*

The specificities of Ladele's case strongly suggest that – given that the employment goalposts were moved around her; that she and Islington (like other councils) had managed to find an acceptable *modus operandi;* that no service users had complained about her; and that the issue had only become a legal case because two colleagues claimed to feel victimised by Ladele's views – in this instance, accommodation could have been reached, and Ladele offered a limited exemption. This will be morally distasteful to some but that is precisely the sense that we should be experiencing in a liberal, plural society: if we are to take freedom seriously, as opposed to secure it for people, views and practices that are broadly similar to our own, then everyone will find themselves legally accommodating practices that they find morally problematic.

As suggested in the previous section, a proportional approach may have been best suited to this case, which is precisely what wasn't used. In the words of the two dissenting judges:

> Ms Ladele did not fail in her duty of discretion: she did not publicly express her beliefs to service users. Her beliefs had no impact on the content of her job, but only on its extent. She never attempted to impose her beliefs on others, nor was she in any way engaged, openly or surreptitiously, in subverting the rights of others. Thus, even if one were to undertake the proportionality exercise referred to in § 106 [in

the European Court's judgement] with reference to whatever legitimate aim the Borough had in view, it follows that the means used were totally disproportionate.[87]

This invariably invites the question about whether religious freedom, therefore, secures exemption from all equality legislation, to which the answer is a clear no. As already mentioned, religious commitment is not a get-out-of-jail-free card. Were Ms Ladele to have been outspoken or offensive in her views, especially towards service users, she should not have been granted an exemption. Had it been completely impossible for Islington Council to have reworked their registrars' rota around her objections, it is unlikely that she should have been granted an exemption. Had Ms Ladele started with her revised duties and then latterly changed her mind, she would not have been granted an exemption. And were she to be applying for the job as registrar now at Islington Council, it seems unlikely that she should have been granted an exemption.

In such a way, it should be clear that articulating a religious belief, however coherent, significant and sincere does not automatically grant an exemption. Many contextual and circumstance-specific issues intervene, not least that of chronology: public employees who have their terms and conditions, even their job descriptions, changed around them have a greater right to exemption than those who are coming to a job for the first time.

Even here, however, the case is not quite cut-and-dried, for although employees do not as a rule have a right to shape job descriptions around themselves, nor does the state have the right to ignore all calls of an applicant's conscience, religious or otherwise, not least because the state is so large an employer in contemporary society. The historian AJP Taylor once famously wrote that until August 1914 a sensible, law-abiding Englishman could pass through life and hardly notice the existence of the state, beyond the post office and the policeman. This is inconceivable today and for this reason it is not just that public sector employers adopt a take-it-or-leave-it approach to applicants. In as far as it is possible, accommodation should be made for people's sincere religious (and other, similar) beliefs, albeit the requirement for such accommodation is weaker than it is for existing employees.

Not surprisingly, therefore, the answer to this final question of religious freedom is again qualified. Equality legislation is an important and valuable contribution to a fair society. However, if it is administered in a "doctrinaire" fashion, or inequitably, or without due attempts at accommodation, or without a sense of proportionality, it risks burdening some in society unnecessarily. This is not the same as saying that religious people are automatically free from the obligations of equality law, but rather that equality law should be made to serve the common good rather than to pursue more limited social agendas.

conclusion

The seven questions posed in the second part of this essay do not exhaust the subjects in which religion and law interact. One might also have asked about the existence and role of 'faith' schools; of religious education within schools; of family law and the relationship between parents and children; of charity law and the concept of the public good; of medical treatment and religious ethics; and so forth.[88]

Nor has the treatment of these seven questions been exhaustive. This volume has been kept deliberately short, partly to avoid scaring readers away, and partly because the intent of the essay has not been to answer questions definitively – were such a thing possible – but to help readers to think about religious freedom from an authentically Christian point of view.

Taken together with the contributions in *Religion and Law*, the first volume in this series, in which legal scholars were able to focus on specific questions, it is hoped that this essay will enable readers to navigate complex and sometimes confusing territory without jettisoning their religious convictions or being compelled to adopt other people's. The territory is, however, changing – indeed it has arguably changed more rapidly over the last 15 years than it did in the previous 50, and it is therefore incumbent on anyone with a live interest in religious freedom to continue to think through the principles and issues at hand with the sensitivity and self-criticism that is essential for this topic.

chapter 2 references

1   http://www.secularism.org.uk/disestablishment.html

2   https://humanism.org.uk/campaigns/secularism/constitutional-reform/

3   Rex Ahdar and Ian Leigh *Religious Freedom in the Liberal State* (Oxford: OUP, 2005) p. 88.

4   Mark Hill, *Ecclesiastical Law*, 3rd ed. (Oxford: Oxford University Press, 2007).

5   See Hill, *Ecclesiastical Law*, para. 2.06.

6   Such as with regard to rights concerning marriage and burial. See Sandberg, *Religion and Law*, p. 78.

7   Denmark has an established Evangelical Lutheran Church which is supported as the state religion, with the government collecting taxes on behalf of the Church, and subsidising clergy salaries and pensions. The Danish National Church has no synod, no legal personality and is not a corporate body. The state Ministry of Ecclesiastical Affairs determines rules concerning membership and the creation of new parishes, and approves the appointment and dismissal of clergy, who have the status of civil servants.

8   Greece has a state church, but this is self-governing and has the status of being a legal person. Articles 33 and 59 of the Constitution require that the president and members of parliament take religious oaths of office (Greek Orthodox by default, though members – but not the president – can take other religious oaths if they request so). Furthermore, Article 16 states that "the development of national and religious consciousness" is part of the government's obligations with regard to education. The Greek government also subsidises the Orthodox Church, including maintaining church buildings and salaries for clergy.

9   Finland maintains two state churches, Evangelical Lutheran and Orthodox, and the state collects taxes on their behalf.

10 In Malta, Catholicism is the state religion, and the constitution gives the church "the duty and right to teach which principles are right and which are wrong."

11 *Darby v Sweden* [1990] ECtHR 24 (No. 11581/85) (23 October 1990) http://www.bailii.org/eu/cases/ECHR/1990/24.html

12 Ahdar and Leigh *Religious Freedom op. cit.*

13 http://www.theguardian.com/world/2013/jun/02/atheists-churches-free-parking As a result of the NSS's threat of legal action, Woking Council amended their policy so that members of other community groups who promote social inclusion and undertake voluntary work may also park free of charge in the Council's car parks. In response, the NSS "postpone[d] its threatened action", at least until it assessed "how the new policy works in practice." http://www.secularism.org.uk/news/2013/08/woking-council-issue-clarification-on-worshippers-parking-policy

14 S. Ferrari, 'Law and Religion in Europe' in I. Christoffersen et al. (eds), *Religion in the 21st Century* (Aldershot: Ashgate, 2010), p. 153

15 http://hudoc.echr.coe.int/sites/eng/pages/search.aspx?i=001-58921#{"itemid":["001-58921"]}

16 Such as to whom exactly the legislation could be applied.

17 Such that the exemption would not hold if a particular appointment could be shown to be improper, the definition of improper including the word 'arbitrary'.

18 http://www.supremecourt.gov/opinions/11pdf/10-553.pdf

19 Or, at least, the core of one type of liberal society. Liberalism has more than one face and can be perfectly happy to impose certain conceptions of the good on the basis that it is through certain forms of coercion that liberty and/or equality are best secured.

20   *Serif v Greece*, para. 53, http://echr.ketse.com/doc/38178.97-en-19991214/view/

21   [Declaration on the Elimination of All Forms of Intolerance and of Discrimination Based on Religion or Belief: http://www.ohchr.org/Documents/ProfessionalInterest/religion.pdf }

22   *Rayburn v General Conference of Seventh Day Adventists*; http://www.leagle.com/decision/19851936772 F2d1164_11761

23   See, for example, *HH Sant Baba Jeet Singh Maharaj v. Eastern Media Group Ltd.* [2010] EWHC (QB) 1294, which speaks of "the well-known principle of English law to the effect that the courts will not attempt to rule upon doctrinal issues or intervene in the regulation or governance of religious groups." [para. 5] http://www.bailii.org/ew/cases/EWHC/QB/2010/1294.html

24   Again, this is most carefully articulated in US jurisprudence for the obvious reason: "The First Amendment… commands civil courts to decide church property disputes without resolving controversies over religious doctrine." *Presbyterian Church v. Hull Church* – 393 U.S. 440 (1969) http://supreme.justia.com/cases/federal/us/393/440/case.html

25   http://www.legislation.gov.uk/ukpga/2010/15/notes/division/3/16/26. Emphases added.

26   Note 796.

27   Ahdar and Leigh, *Religious Freedom* op. cit. p. 395.

28   http://rowanwilliams.archbishopofcanterbury.org/articles.php/1137/

29   "A Code of Canon Law is absolutely necessary for the Church. Since the Church is established in the form of a social and visible unit, it needs rules, so that its hierarchical and organic structure may be visible; that its exercise of the functions divinely entrusted to it, particularly of sacred power and of the administration of the sacraments, is properly ordered; that the mutual relationships of Christ's faithful are reconciled in justice based on charity, with the rights of each safeguarded and defined; and lastly, that the common initiatives which are undertaken so that Christian life may be ever more perfectly carried out, are supported, strengthened and promoted by canonical laws." http://www.ourladyswarriors.org/canon/promulgate.htm

30   Maleiha Malik, 'Religious Minorities and Law: Understanding Minority Legal Orders in the UK' in Nick Spencer (ed.) *Religion and Law* (London: Theos, 2012) p. 32.

31   Alan Johnson, 'The slaughter and torture of Christians: not a priority for the Government, Labour or DfID', *The Telegraph*, 9 December 2013. For a parliamentary debate on the issue see http://www.publications.parliament.uk/pa/cm201314/cmhansrd/cm131203/debtext/131203-0003.htm

32   http://www.secularism.org.uk/news/2013/12/non-religious-suffer-discrimination-or-persecution-in-most-countries-of-the-world-new-report-finds

33   Employment Equality (Religion or Belief) Regulations 2003, Reg 2(1).

34   *Williams v South Central Limited*.

35   *Baggs v Fudge*.

36   This definition is now to be found in Equality Act 2010, s10.

37   House of Lords Debate, 13 July 2005 col 1109-1110.

38   Russell Sandberg, 'A Question of Belief' in *Religion and Law*, pp. 52-53.

39   *R v Secretary of State for Education and Employment and others ex parte Williamson*

40   *R v Secretary of State for Education*, para 23.

41   *R v Secretary of State for Education*, para 23.

42   *R v Secretary of State for Education*, para 57.

43   *Grainger PLC v Nicholson*.

44 *Grainger PLC v Nicholson*, para. 24.

45 *Whaley v Lord Advocate*, para. 18: "[Looking at it] objectively, hunting with hounds is carried on mainly for pleasure and relaxation for those who take part in it… The current jurisprudence does not support the proposition that a person's belief in his right to engage in an activity which he carries on for pleasure or recreation, however fervent or passionate, can be equated with beliefs of the kind that are protected by article 9.

46 *Hashman v Milton Park (Dorset) Ltd*, Employment tribunal Case Number: 3105555/2009 (31 January 2011).

47 *Greater Manchester Police Authority v Power* [2009] EAT 0434/09/DA (12 November 2009).

48 *Maistry v The BBC*. Employment tribunal Pre-Hearing Review Case Number: 1213142/2010 (14 February 2011). At para 17-18.

49 *Maistry v The BBC*, para 28.

50 *Unison v Kelly*, Employment tribunal Case Number 2203854/08 (22 December 2009).

51 Russell Sandberg, 'A Question of Belief' in *Religion and Law*, p. 57.

52 I am grateful to Julian Rivers for making this point to me.

53 Corinna Adam, 'Protecting Our Lord', in *New Statesman*, 15 July 1977, repr. 13 February 2006, http://www.newstatesman.com/node/152583

54 http://www.legislation.gov.uk/ukpga/2006/1/contents

55 Ahdar and Leigh, *Religious Freedom*, pp. 458-59.

56 http://www.bailii.org/eu/cases/ECHR/2013/37.html

57 As the National Secular Society memorably put it in an article of the same title, "BA needs defending from religious zealots, not the other way round"; http://www.secularism.org.uk/baneedsdefendingfromreligiouszea.html

58 *Amicus* case, [2004] IRLR 430, 438, para 44, quoted in http://www.publications.parliament.uk/pa/ld200405/ldjudgmt/jd050224/will-3.htm

59 *Oregon* case 494 US 872, 888, footnote 4, quoted in http://www.publications.parliament.uk/pa/ld200405/ldjudgmt/jd050224/will-3.htm

60 One is reminded of the episode of the BBC's political comedy, *The Thick of It*, when the minister, Hugh Abbot, has made up his mind on an issue having spoken to a policy expert. Unfortunately, his decision is at odds with his government's policy. The party spin doctor, Malcolm Tucker, tells him that he has spoken to "the wrong expert" and that he should have spoken to "the right expert". When Abbot asks who this is right expert is, Tucker says that he doesn't know but he can find Abbot one by the afternoon. Matters of religious expertise are, hopefully, not as pliable – or cynical – as this, but are sufficiently complex and involve to allow for a range of legitimate expert opinions.

61 http://www.casas.org.uk/papers/pdfpapers/cremationjudgement.pdf

62 http://www.bailii.org/ew/cases/EWCA/Civ/2009/1357.html para 52.

63 Paragraph 88, quoted in *Mba v Mayor and Burgesses of the London Borough of Merton*; http://www.bailii.org/ew/cases/EWCA/Civ/2013/1562.html

64 "After the most anxious consideration, I have come to the conclusion that, in all the circumstances of this case, and notwithstanding the legal errors to which I have referred, the decision of the E[mployment] T[ribunal] that the imposition of the PCP [provision, criterion or practice] was proportionate was 'plainly and unarguably right'. In truth, once Mrs Mba failed to establish the more favourable terms of the contract for which she had contended and the Council had established that there was really no viable or practicable alternative way of running Brightwell effectively, there was

only ever going to be one outcome to this case. The legal error can have made no difference." Para. 24.

65 [2007] EWCA Civ 893: http://www.bailii.org/cgi-bin/markup.cgi?doc=/ew/cases/EWHC/Admin/2007/1736.html&query=Shambo&method=boolean

66 *R (on the Application of Ghai) v Newcastle City Council*: http://www.bailii.org/ew/cases/EWCA/Civ/2010/59.html; http://www.casas.org.uk/papers/pdfpapers/cremationjudgement.pdf

67 http://www.casas.org.uk/papers/pdfpapers/cremationjudgement.pdf, para. 105.

68 http://www.bailii.org/eu/cases/ECHR/1978/7.html

69 http://www.bailii.org/cgi-bin/markup.cgi?doc=/ew/cases/EWHC/Admin/2007/1698.html&query=Playfoot&method=boolean

70 http://www.bailii.org/ew/cases/EWHC/Admin/2008/1865.html

71 http://hudoc.echr.coe.int/sites/fra/pages/search.aspx?i=001-115881#{"itemid":["001-115881"]}

72 http://www.bailii.org/uk/cases/UKHL/2006/15.html

73 http://uk.practicallaw.com/7-375-8114?service=employment

74 http://www.bailii.org/ew/cases/EWCA/Civ/2005/932.html

75 Megan Pearson, 'Proportionality: A way forward for resolving religious claims?' in *Religion and Law*, (ed.) Nick Spencer (London: Theos, 2012), pp. 35-42.

76 http://www.bailii.org/uk/cases/UKHL/2005/15.html

77 This was "a combination of the kameeze, a sleeveless smock-like dress with a square neckline, revealing the wearer's collar and tie, with the shalwar, loose trousers, tapering at the ankles. A long-sleeved white shirt is worn beneath the kameeze and, save in hot weather, a uniform long-sleeved school jersey is worn on top." Para. 6.

78 A similar point could be made of the Royal Devon and Exeter NHS Trust, which was prepared to permit Ms Chaplin to wear pinned cross on a her lapel in place of the crucifix chain.

79 Megan Pearson, 'Proportionality', p. 37.

80 Although this is an asymmetric form of reasonable accommodation, whereby favourable treatment afforded to a disabled employee cannot be used as the basis for a claim by a disgruntled able-bodied employee. By contrast, religious discrimination is symmetrical: it protects both religion and belief and a lack of religion and belief. Gibson, 'The God "Dilution"?', p. 593.

81 Gibson, 'The God "Dilution"?', p. 596.

82 Gibson, 'The God "Dilution"?', p. 596.

83 Gibson, 'The God "Dilution"?', pp. 608, 611.

84 http://www.equalityhumanrights.com/legal-and-policy/human-rights-legal-powers/legal-intervention-on-religion-or-belief-rights-2011/

85 Thomas Hammarberg, *Opinion of the Commissioner for Human Rights on National Structures for Promoting Equality*; https://wcd.coe.int/ViewDoc.jsp?id=1761031

86 Case of Eweida and Others v. The United Kingdom (Applications nos. 48420/10, 59842/10, 51671/10 and 36516/10).

87 Case of *Eweida and Others v. The United Kingdom* (Applications nos. 48420/10, 59842/10, 51671/10 and 36516/10); Joint Partly Dissenting Opinion of Judges VUČINIĆ and DE GAETANO, para. 7.

88 Some of these are dealt with in part III of Adhar and Leigh, *Religious Freedom*.